DEVELOPING YOUR EMOTIONAL INTELLIGENCE SKILLS

April 2021-November 2022 Editions

EI Skills Group notes the following errors in the 2021 edition of Developing Your Emotional Intelligence Skills.

1. *On page 14, in the image, the words "PLEASANT" and "UNPLEASANT" should be reversed (UNPLEASANT begins at 0 and PLEASANT ends at 10).*

2. *On page 16, in image, the words "PLEASANT" and "UNPLEASANT" should be reversed (UNPLEASANT begins at 0 and PLEASANT ends at 10).*

3. *On page 43, in image, the words "PLEASANT" and "UNPLEASANT" should be reversed (UNPLEASANT begins at 0 and PLEASANT ends at 10).*

4. *On page 151, in image the words "PLEASANT" and "UNPLEASANT" should be reversed (UNPLEASANT begins at 0 and PLEASANT ends at 10).*

Issue Date: December 4, 2022

DEVELOPING YOUR EMOTIONAL INTELLIGENCE SKILLS

SKILL BUILDING WORKBOOK

Based on the books, *A Leader's Guide to Solving Challenges with Emotional Intelligence* and *The Educator's Practical Guide to Emotional Intelligence*

David R. Caruso, PhD   Lisa T. Rees, PCC, MPA

CONTENTS

INTRODUCTION 3

HOW TO USE THIS WORKBOOK 4

ORIENTATION 6

FIRST ABILITY: MAP EMOTION 14

SECOND ABILITY: MATCH EMOTION 43

THIRD ABILITY: MEANING OF EMOTION 67

FOURTH ABILITY: MOVE EMOTIONS 89

EMOTIONAL INTELLIGENCEBLUEPRINT 115

COMMITMENTS AND CONCLUSIONS 147

APPENDICES 150

ABOUT THE AUTHORS 154

ACKNOWLEDGEMENTS 156

Developing Your Emotional Intelligence Skills by David R. Caruso and Lisa T. Rees

Copyright © Caruso and Rees 2021
All rights reserved

ISBN: 978-1-945028-34-2

Although the authors have made every effort to ensure that the information in this book was correct at press time, the authors and publisher do not assume and hereby disclaim any liability to any party for any loss, damage, or disruption caused by errors or omissions, whether such errors or omissions result from negligence, accident, or any other cause.

Please visit EISkillsGroup.com

INTRODUCTION

We wrote the book, **A Leader's Guide to Solving Challenges with Emotional Intelligence**, for leaders who want to enhance their emotional intelligence skills, develop stronger relationships with others, and achieve goals through engaged collaboration. The book is based on the concept that emotions are data, emotions can be intelligent and emotional intelligence is a hard skill which effective leaders must develop. This workbook is a culmination of our over 35 years of combined experience teaching, practicing, and coaching emotional intelligence skills. Many of our class participants, clients, and Emotional Intelligence (EI) practitioners have requested we develop a skill-building workbook, and after many years, we are pleased to offer this workbook.

Many view emotions as something to be controlled, but few realize emotions, all emotions, can be adaptive, helpful, and "smart." We know emotions help leaders build trust, engage employees, and can be used to achieve positive organizational goals. We also know emotions, when not managed intelligently, can create toxic work environments, break down communication and lead to falling short of personal and professional goals.

This workbook is for leaders, aspiring leaders, educators, coaches, and others who want to strengthen their skills in leveraging emotions to build healthy, thriving relationships and organizations. The exercises in this workbook will help you practice each of the four emotional intelligence abilities – Map, Match, Meaning and Move, as well as exercises on how to use all four abilities in what we call the "Emotional Intelligence Blueprint." We also included exercises to complete as a group, which may be useful to facilitators, teachers, coaches, and leaders who want to help others develop their emotional intelligence skills.

Once you complete the workbook, you will have concrete ways to raise your EI awareness, leverage emotions to reach your goals and learn effective strategies to successfully navigate emotions. Emotions, after all, are what make life worth living and, if used intelligently, can help you make better decisions and be more effective. We hope you embrace emotions and see them as a help and not a hindrance when striving to reach your personal and professional goals.

We are committed to your continued learning and development. Please do not hesitate to contact us at blueprint@eiskills.com with any questions you have or support you need. Best of luck in your continued success!

Many thanks,
David R. Caruso, New Haven, Connecticut
Lisa T. Rees, Burlington, Vermont

HOW TO USE THIS WORKBOOK

We recommend starting from the beginning of the workbook as each EI ability builds upon the prior one. The following is an overview of each ability and its importance.

MAP EMOTIONS BY USING THE MOOD MAP TO ACCURATELY GAUGE YOUR EMOTIONS AND THOSE OF OTHERS.

- COMMUNICATE MEANING
- PICK UP ON CUES
- READ THE ROOM
- IDENTIFY PROBLEMS

MATCH EMOTIONS TO THE TASK TO ACHIEVE SUCCESSFUL OUTCOMES AND BUILD RELATIONSHIPS.

- MATCH EMOTIONS TO TASK TO ACCOMPLISH GOALS
- MATCH EMOTIONS OF OTHERS TO DEMONSTRATE EMOTIONAL
- CREATE CONNECTIONS
- INSPIRE AND MOTIVATE

MEANING OF EMOTIONS ARE IDENTIFIED AND ANALYZED TO BETTER UNDERSTAND THEIR CAUSE AND PREDICT HOW THEY WILL CHANGE.

- COMMUNICATE MEANING
- "FIGURE PEOPLE OUT"
- PREDICT EMOTIONAL OUTCOMES
- UNDERSTAND CAUSES OF EMOTIONS TO ENHANCE DECISION MAKING

MOVE EMOTIONS, BOTH YOURS AND OTHERS' TO YIELD DECISION MAKING

- STRATEGIES TO MANAGE YOUR EMOTIONS
- METHODS TO MANAGE OTHERS' EMOTIONS
- PSYCH PEOPLE UP, CALM OTHERS DOWN
- BE MORE RESILIENT AND COPE BETTER WITH STRESS

HOW TO USE THIS WORKBOOK

Each section of the workbook includes exercises to help deepen your understanding of each ability. Some of the exercises require participation from others, but most can be done on your own. We recommend practicing in areas where you show strength, as well as areas that may need developing. The key is not to move too quickly through the exercises, but rather to be deliberate in your practice so they become a habit. As you will learn, **mapping, matching,** understanding **meaning,** and **moving** emotions is challenging – especially under stress. However, with practice you will notice the importance of emotions and develop effective ways to use them to reach personal and professional goals.

At the end of the workbook we combine all the abilities into an EI Blueprint and provide exercises on how to use the 4 M's to solve difficult leadership challenges. We also include detailed step by step instructions on how to build your own EI Blueprint. Using these steps will help you see your challenges from different perspectives, giving you the ability to reframe your challenges into tangible, realistic opportunities.

A note about the four abilities - These abilities may seem familiar to you. They are the four abilities from the Mayer-Salovey ability model of emotional intelligence that we relabeled to make them, hopefully, a bit more memorable. Another model you may be familiar with, called RULER, is also based on the Mayer-Salovey model, and uses slightly different terms. The below table lists these different terms to help you understand the source labeling of the four abilities.

The Four M's	Mayer - Salovey Model	Ruler
Map	Perceive	Recognize/ Express
Match	Facilitate / Use	N/A
Meaning	Understand	Understand/ Label
Move	Manage	Regulate

ORIENTATION

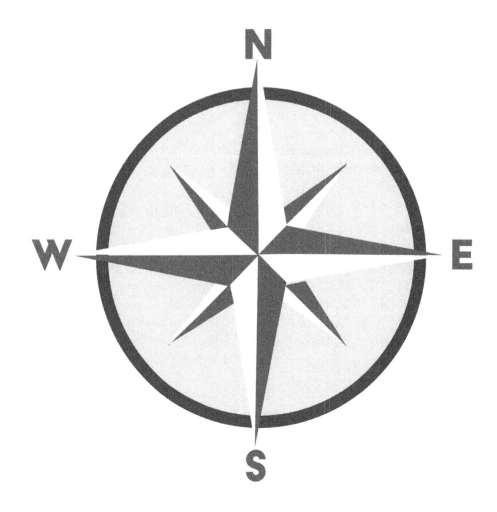

Most professional development programs include learning about emotional intelligence, but few fully understand its importance in life. We go about our day experiencing emotions continuously and some may find it an inconvenience, while others recognize how important emotions are to building trust, strengthening relationships, and successfully achieving goals. The following Orientation exercises will help you better understand how EI shows up in life and how your EI ability can help or hinder your work.

ORIENTATION EXERCISE 1: RAISING EI AWARENESS

Learning Objective: Emotional intelligence is critical to leadership and can be used effectively in many situations, both in and out of work. This exercise helps raise awareness of which activities are enhanced by EI and highlights areas where you may want to intentionally practice EI to achieve more effective outcomes. (Note: The list of activities in the below table were selected based on more than 25 years of research that shows when EI is practiced while performing these activities, the outcome yielded more positive results.)

Instructions:
1. Review the common activities in the table below and indicate how relevant these activities are and how often you perform these tasks in a week.

2. After marking the relevance and frequency for each activity, answer the related questions.

Activity/ Task	Relevant to Me?		If yes, indicate how often you perform this activity		
	YES	NO	O Once	O Twice	O More than Twice
Lead a Group			O Once	O Twice	O More than Twice
Serve on a Team			O Once	O Twice	O More than Twice
Form Relationships			O Once	O Twice	O More than Twice
Handle Conflict			O Once	O Twice	O More than Twice
Manage Stress			O Once	O Twice	O More than Twice
Achieve Goals Through Consensus			O Once	O Twice	O More than Twice
Have Empathy			O Once	O Twice	O More than Twice
Read People More Accurately			O Once	O Twice	O More than Twice
Express Emotions			O Once	O Twice	O More than Twice

Discovery Questions:

WHAT ACTIVITIES DO YOU PERFORM MOST FREQUENTLY?

WHICH ACTIVITIES OR AREAS ARE MOST IMPORTANT TO YOU?

LOOKING AT BOTH THE FREQUENCY AND IMPORTANCE OF EACH ACTIVITY, CHOOSE ONE AND INDICATE WHAT IMPACT ENHANCING YOUR EI SKILLS MIGHT HAVE IN YOUR ABILITY TO DO THIS ACTIVITY BETTER. WHAT IMPACT WILL PRACTICING EI WHILE DOING THIS ACTIVITY HAVE ON YOU AND OTHERS?

Discovery Questions:

ORIENTATION EXERCISE 2: DANGERS OF OVERCONFIDENCE

Learning Objective: Most people, according to one study conducted in 2014, overestimate their EI ability*. And even more interestingly, they are less likely to be interested in EI skill development and more likely to question the importance and relevance of this skill set. This exercise helps to identify common pitfalls people encounter when they are not aware of EI's importance and relevance in day to day interactions with others.

Instructions:

1. Answer each question by recalling a time when you may have underestimated the impact emotions had on the situation.

2. Challenge yourself to go deeper and reflect on what happened, how people felt and the impact your actions had in improving or making the situation worse.

3. After answering the questions below, take time to journal what you will do in the future to avoid overlooking the importance of EI and how you will integrate it in your words and actions.

RECALL A TIME WHEN YOU MISREAD ANOTHER PERSON'S EMOTIONAL EXPRESSION. WHAT WAS THE SITUATION? WHAT WAS THE IMPACT? HOW COULD A MORE ACCURATE READ HAVE HELPED?

RECALL A TIME WHEN YOU WERE SURPRISED BY ANOTHER PERSON'S REACTION TO WHAT YOU DID OR SAID. WHAT WAS THE SITUATION? WHAT WAS THE IMPACT? HOW COULD A MORE ACCURATE PREDICTION HAVE HELPED?

---

*Sheldon, O. J., Dunning, D., & Ames, D. R. (2014). Emotionally unskilled, unaware, and uninterested in learning more: reactions to feedback about deficits in emotional intelligence. Journal of Applied Psychology, 99, 125-137. http://dx.doi.org/10.1037/a0034138

RECALL A TIME WHEN YOU HAD A PROBLEM EMOTIONALLY "GETTING" OR CONNECTING WITH SOMEONE. WHAT WAS THE SITUATION? WHAT WAS THE IMPACT? HOW COULD A CLOSER RELATIONSHIP HAVE HELPED?

RECALL A TIME WHEN YOU TRIED TO HELP RESOLVE A CONFLICT BUT FAILED. WHAT WAS THE SITUATION? WHAT WAS THE IMPACT? HOW COULD A MORE ACCURATE READ OF THE SITUATION HAVE HELPED?

REVIEW YOUR PREVIOUS RESPONSES. WHAT THEMES OR TRENDS DO YOU NOTICE? WHAT DO YOU SEE AS A PATTERN IN HOW YOU DEAL WITH EMOTIONS? IN WHAT AREAS HAVE YOU PERHAPS OVERESTIMATED YOUR EI ABILITY?

NOW THAT YOU HAVE IDENTIFIED TRENDS, THEMES, OR PATTERNS WHEN YOU DO NOT USE EI, WHAT WILL YOU DO DIFFERENTLY TO CONSIDER EI AND YOUR ABILITY BEFORE ENGAGING IN A CONVERSATION WITH OTHERS OR MAKING DECISIONS?

ORIENTATION EXERCISE 3: RAISING EI AWARENESS

Learning Objective: Emotional Intelligence, done well, helps individuals and teams achieve more successful outcomes in life. Therefore, it is important to understand how your EI skills impact the work you do every day. This exercise is for those who have taken an ability based EI assessment (e.g., MSCEIT), and want to better understand how their EI skills help or hinder in certain circumstances. (If you would like to take the MSCEIT and receive individual feedback, please contact us for more information.)

Instructions:

1. Review and indicate your MSCEIT results for each of the four abilities in the table.

2. After reviewing, answer the reflective questions at the end of this exercise.

MSCEIT Ability	Score	MSCEIT Range
Perceive (Map)		
Facilitation (Match)		
Understanding (Meaning)		
Manage (Move)		

REFLECTING ON YOUR PERCEIVE (MAP) SCORE, HOW MIGHT YOUR EI RESULTS IMPACT YOUR WORK?

REFLECTING ON YOUR FACILITATION (MATCH) SCORE, HOW MIGHT YOUR EI RESULTS IMPACT YOUR WORK?

REFLECTING ON YOUR UNDERSTAND (MEANING) SCORE, HOW MIGHT YOUR EI RESULTS IMPACT YOUR WORK?

REFLECTING ON YOUR MANAGE (MOVE) SCORE, HOW MIGHT YOUR EI RESULTS IMPACT YOUR WORK?

HOW MIGHT YOUR EI RESULTS **POSITIVELY IMPACT** YOU AS YOU WORK ON **YOUR OWN**?

HOW MIGHT YOUR EI RESULTS **POSITIVELY IMPACT** YOU AS YOU WORK **WITH OTHERS**?

HOW MIGHT YOUR EI RESULTS **INTERFERE** AS YOU WORK ON **YOUR OWN**?

HOW MIGHT YOUR EI RESULTS **INTERFERE** WITH YOUR WORK **WITH OTHERS**?

BELOW, LIST THE ABILITY YOU WANT TO PRACTICE AND FOCUS ON FIRST AND WHY IT'S IMPORTANT TO YOU.

FIRST ABILITY: MAP EMOTION

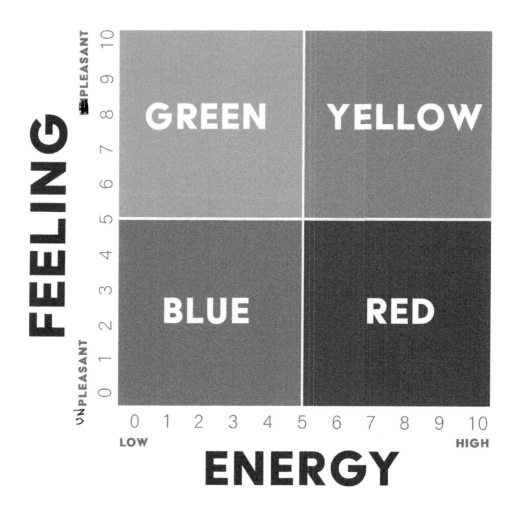

In life, we make hundreds of decisions every day. To make the best decision, we use a myriad of sources, but few consider one of the most important sources of data, our emotions. Accurately identifying emotions is the first of the four EI abilities and, therefore, it is critical to do it well. Emotions contain a wealth of information that help us think more clearly, help teams be more cohesive and collaborate, and build trust. Once we correctly identify the emotions we and others are experiencing, we can then determine if they are the best emotions to support and reach our goals. The following Map exercises will help you accurately identify emotions so you can use these "data" to help guide your decision making.

MAP EXERCISE 1: MAP YOUR EMOTIONS

Learning Objective: Awareness of basic emotions is the beginning point of emotional intelligence. This exercise helps you monitor your emotions, accurately identify them, and track how they change throughout the day.

Instructions:

1. Make a copy of the Mood Map* (see next page).

2. Consider how much energy you have right at this moment. Use a 0 to 10-point energy scale with 0 being completely restful and relaxed, almost asleep, and 10 as being highly energized. Select a number that best represents your current energy level.

3. Next, how pleasant or unpleasant are you feeling right now? Again, calibrate the 0 to 10 scale where 0 is the 'lowest' or most unpleasant feelings you are experiencing and 10 being the most pleasant you are experiencing. Select the number representing your current feeling.

4. Now, take the two numbers (energy and feeling) and plot them on the Mood Map with the time of entry.

5. Record your entries on the Mood Map several times throughout the day (upon waking, mid-day, late afternoon, evening). At the end of the day, draw a line between the entries showing how your emotion may have changed throughout the day.

6. Take time to reflect on how your emotions shifted during the day and how you were accurately able to identify them.

7. Do this exercise several days in a row to find patterns in your emotional state.

*Note on our terms: You may be familiar with the "Mood Meter". The Mood Meter was formally introduced in the 2004 book The Emotionally Intelligent Manager by David Caruso and Peter Salovey. The x-axis was for Pleasantness and the y-axis for Energy. Later, the Mood Meter used a -5 to +5 scale (Brackett, Caruso & Stern, 2011). The Mood Map switches the axes since most people start with Energy when mapping their feelings and returns to the 0 to 10 scale to highlight the point that feelings are not "negative." Finally, we use the term "Map" which seems more accurate when plotting a point using x- and y-coordinates.

MOOD MAP TEMPLATE

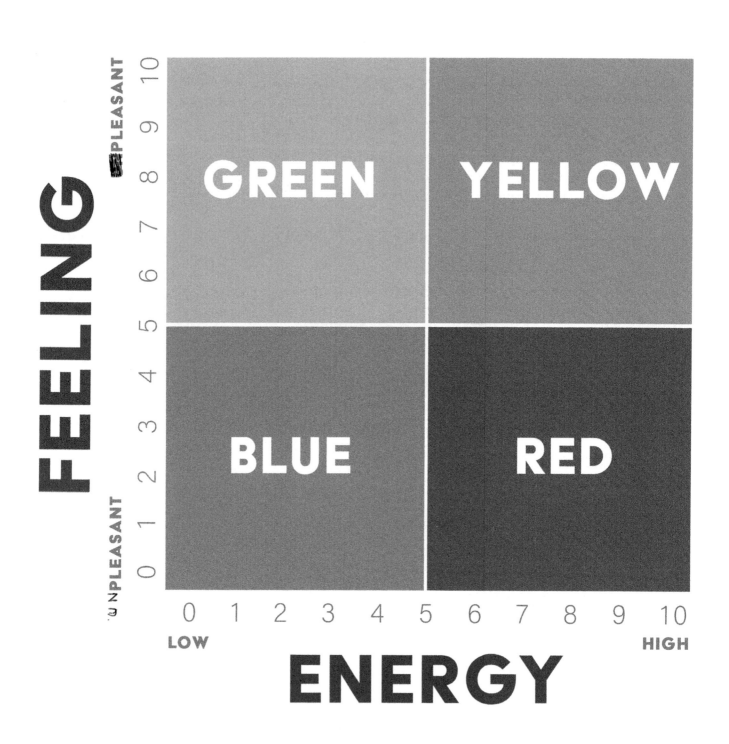

MAP EXERCISE 2: MAP OTHER'S EMOTIONS

Learning Objective: Successfully identifying and mapping emotions is critical when interacting with others. How others feel impacts how they behave and influences their thinking. Therefore, having complete and accurate emotional data will help guide your decision making and result in better interactions with others. This exercise helps you better identify how other people are feeling.

Instructions:
1. Make a copy of the Mood Map (see Exercise 1).

2. Select a friend, relative, or colleague to observe.

3. Based on your observations, plot the other person's mood on the Mood Map.

4. At the bottom of the Mood Map page, indicate the observed person, situation, date and time of the entry.

5. Approach your target and explain the purpose of the exercise and the Mood Map (have a blank map available). Ask the person where they would place themselves.

6. Compare your entry with their entry and see how close your ratings are to each other. Share where you placed them, and why, and ask how accurate you were.

7. Complete the Discovery Questions to clarify discrepancies.

Discovery Questions:
Reflect on how you rated the person's emotion and how they rated themselves. If your ratings were the same or close, congratulations – you were able to accurately identify someone else's emotions by observation! However, oftentimes, we may not be accurate, so let's find out why.

WHAT OBSERVATIONS OF FACIAL EXPRESSIONS AND OTHER NON-VERBAL CUES DID YOU USE TO MAP THEIR EMOTION?

HOW DID YOU INFER FROM THE SITUATION OR CONTEXT HOW THE TARGET MIGHT HAVE FELT?

WHAT OTHER "DATA" DID YOU USE TO IDENTIFY THEIR EMOTION?

WHAT ASSUMPTIONS DID YOU PERHAPS MAKE THAT LED YOU TO THE EMOTION YOU IDENTIFIED?

WHAT DID YOU LEARN FROM YOUR OBSERVATION THAT WILL HELP YOU MORE ACCURATELY IDENTIFY EMOTIONS IN OTHERS?

MAP EXERCISE 3: EMOTIONAL MATCH GAME

Learning Objective: Accurately identifying emotions seems like an easy task, but sometimes we overanalyze or overlook what is in front of us. We may also project our own feelings onto others as we analyze someone else's emotions. A person's face reveals certain physical characteristics that are displayed when a person experiences a specific emotion. This exercise helps you become more accurate in identifying facial expressions in pictures.

Instructions:

1. Have on hand a deck of Emotions Flashcards available at www.picturemypicture.com or search for "emotional expressions."

2. Deal out 10 emotion cards face up.

3. Study each face and determine which of the 10 cards belong to the same emotion "family" (See Table 2. Emotion Words at Work in our book, **A Leader's Guide to Solving Challenges with Emotional Intelligence**.)

4. Place each card in its correct emotion "family."

5. Deal out another 10 emotion cards, face up, and repeat step 3.

6. Repeat step 5 until all the cards are in the correct "family" and make a stack for each one.

7. Next, take each stack of cards and flip the faces over to reveal the emotion. Does each emotion belong to the correct "family"?

8. If not, debrief the exercise using the Discovery Questions.

Discovery Questions:

HOW DID THIS EXERCISE GO? WAS IT DIFFICULT OR EASY TO IDENTIFY THE EMOTIONS AND PUT THEM IN LIKE FAMILIES OF EMOTIONS? WHY OR WHY NOT?

WERE THERE ANY EMOTIONS YOU CONFUSED FOR ANOTHER AND WHAT DO YOU FEEL CAUSED YOU TO DO SO?

WHAT STRATEGIES WILL YOU USE TO ACCURATELY IDENTIFY A PERSON'S FACIAL EXPRESSIONS GOING FORWARD?

MAP EXERCISE 4: EMOTIONAL TEAM BUILDING

• Group Activity •

Learning Objective: Each person you work with has their own way of expressing emotion. It is important to accurately identify emotions in others to help inform how their emotional state may influence their decision making and behaviors. Oftentimes, we rely on words to indicate emotion, however, it is equally important to identify emotion through body language. This exercise strengthens your ability to accurately identify emotions with others without words.

Instructions:

1. Have on hand a deck of Emotions Flashcards (available at www.picturemypicture.com).

2. Select 5-10 volunteers willing to act out an emotion with one of them being you.

3. Each volunteer picks a card from the deck of emotion cards and has one minute to demonstrate the emotion, without using words.

4. The rest of the team guesses what emotion is being displayed or after one-minute, the participant will share the emotion they were trying to display.

5. Once all volunteers have gone, answer the discovery questions.

Discovery Questions:

> HOW GOOD WERE YOU AT EXPRESSING THE EMOTION?

WHAT DID YOU DO TO CREATE THE EXPRESSION?

HOW GENUINELY DID YOU FEEL YOU EXPRESSED THE EMOTION? WHAT DID YOU FIND DIFFICULT, OR EASY, ABOUT EXPRESSING THE EMOTION?

WERE CERTAIN EMOTIONS MORE DIFFICULT TO IDENTIFY/EXPRESS THAN OTHERS?

HOW ACCURATE WERE YOU AT IDENTIFYING (MAP) OTHERS' EMOTIONS? WHAT CUES DID YOU USE TO DETECT THEIR EMOTION?

WERE CERTAIN EMOTIONS MORE DIFFICULT TO IDENTIFY/EXPRESS THAN OTHERS?

HOW ACCURATE WERE YOU AT IDENTIFYING (MAP) OTHERS' EMOTIONS? WHAT CUES DID YOU USE TO DETECT THEIR EMOTION?

HOW ACCURATE DID YOU FEEL THEY PORTRAYED THEIR EMOTION? IS THIS HOW THEY NORMALLY DISPLAY THIS EMOTION AT WORK? WHY OR WHY NOT?

RECALLING THIS EXERCISE, WHAT WILL YOU DO DIFFERENTLY, OR CONTINUE DOING, THE NEXT TIME YOU HAVE TO IDENTIFY SOMEONE'S EMOTION?

MAP EXERCISE 5: VOICE INFLECTION

• Group Activity •

Learning Objective: Voice inflection is an interesting way to convey emotions. With today's modern technology and environment, we frequently communicate by video and phone. Therefore, it is important to pick up on verbal emotional cues that may not be as evident as when we are face to face. This exercise allows you to practice voice inflection and tone to strengthen your ability to communicate emotion when speaking.

Instructions:

1. Select a person to assist you with this exercise. This person will listen as you read the below statement several times as you convey a different emotion (happiness, frustration, surprise, boredom, contempt) each time. You will ask the listener to guess which emotion you were trying to convey after you read the statement.

2. Read the following non-emotional statement, emoting happiness throughout the entire text*:

   "The U.S. Department of Agriculture provides economic analyses and data on vegetables and pulses for the fresh market and for processing use, including: Current and historical data on supply, use, value, prices, and trade for the sector and for individual commodities; Bimonthly outlook reports that provide current intelligence and forecasts on changing conditions in the U.S. vegetable and pulses sector; In-depth analyses of production, consumption, global production and trade, prices, and conditions and events affecting the vegetable and pulse sector and specific commodities." (Text analysis: https://natural-language-understanding-demo.ng.bluemix.net/)

3. After you read the statement emoting happiness, ask the other person to write down their guess of what you were emoting.

4. Choose the next emotion, frustration, and read the statement again.

5. After reading the statement with a different emotion, have the person write down their guess.

6. Continue the same process, emoting the remaining emotions (surprise, boredom, contempt).

7. After all statements are read, reveal the answers of the emotion you were trying to emote for each reading and see how many they got right.

8. If you want to challenge yourself even further, try this exercise with two additional people and see if they can get all five emotions correct!

9. After completing the exercise, answer the Discovery Questions.

*This text was selected as the emotions detected by a computer program are negligible: Joy .11, Anger .05, Disgust .03, Sadness .07, Fear .04.

OUT OF THE FIVE READINGS, WHICH EMOTION DID YOUR PARTNER GUESS CORRECTLY?

WHICH EMOTIONS WERE MORE DIFFICULT TO EMOTE AND WHY?

WHAT EMOTION(S) DID YOUR PARTNER GUESS INCORRECTLY? IF YOU DID THIS EXERCISE WITH OTHERS, WHAT SIMILARITIES OR DISSIMILARITIES EXISTED BETWEEN THE RESPONSES? WHAT CAUSED THE SIMILARITY OR DISSIMILARITY?

ASK YOUR PARTNER(S) WHAT YOU COULD HAVE DONE TO MORE ACCURATELY EXPRESS EMOTIONS WHEN YOU SPEAK?

MAP EXERCISE 6: EMOTIONS AND THE BODY

Learning Objective: Emotions manifest in the body through physiological responses. Emotions can appear in different locations, with different levels of intensity, and can even appear as colors. Tuning into our bodies is critical in identifying what emotions we are feeling. This exercise helps raise your awareness of where and how emotions show up for you, and how they typically manifest in others.

Note: This exercise is based on the research of Nummenmaa et al and can be read at https://www.pnas.org/content/111/2/646.

Instructions:
1. View the emotions in the first column in the table.

2. For each emotion indicate where in your body this emotion resides. For example, perhaps when you experience love, you feel it in your chest.

3. Next indicate any color you associate with this emotion. For example, you may see love as yellow and red like a fire.

4. Under the feeling column, list any words you associate that emotion with. For example, love may feel warm and sweet.

5. If you have difficulty recreating the emotion, come back to this exercise after you experience the emotion in real time, and complete the entry for that emotion.

6. After completing the table, answer the Discovery Questions.

7. If you would like to view how others experience emotions in their body and in what colors, visit: https://www.pnas.org/content/pnas/111/2/646/F2.large.jpg.

EMOTIONS	WHERE IN MY BODY?	ANY COLOR?	HOW DOES IT FEEL?
Envy			
Happiness			
Neutral			
Anger			
Disgust			
Pride			
Sadness			
Contempt			
Surprise			
Love			
Fear			
Depression			
Shame			
EMOTIONS	WHERE IN MY BODY?	ANY COLOR?	HOW DOES IT FEEL?

Discovery Questions:

WHAT EMOTIONS WERE THE EASIEST TO IDENTIFY IN YOUR BODY AND WHY?

WHAT EMOTIONS WERE MORE DIFFICULT TO IDENTIFY IN YOUR BODY AND WHY?

WHEN THINKING ABOUT YOUR EMOTIONS, WHAT EMOTIONS DO YOU FEEL MOST OFTEN?

HOW AND WHEN DO YOU NOTICE EMOTIONS IN YOUR BODY?

WHAT CAN YOU DO TO BECOME MORE AWARE OF WHERE YOU FEEL EMOTIONS IN YOUR BODY?

IF YOU REVIEWED THE RESEARCH DIAGRAM OF WHERE PEOPLE FEEL EMOTION AND THE ASSOCIATED COLOR, WHAT RESPONSES WERE MOST LIKE YOUR OWN? WHICH ONES WERE MOST DISSIMILAR? WHAT EMOTIONS DID NOT MAKE SENSE TO YOU?

Now **you** try it!

Get out your crayons or markers! Choose a few emotions and use the figures below. Indicate where you feel this emotion and whether it is less or more intense and a colder (use blues) or a warmer (use reds) feeling. Then compare to the figure from the research study.

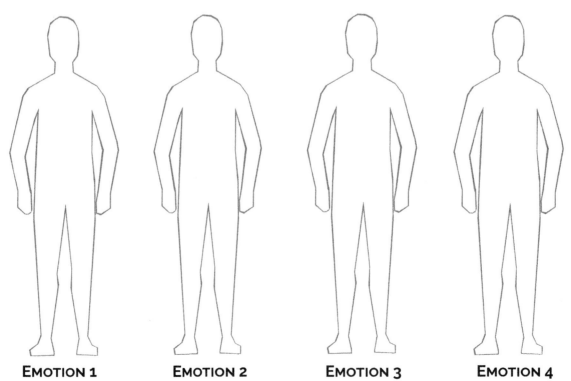

EMOTION 1   EMOTION 2   EMOTION 3   EMOTION 4

MAP EXERCISE 7: EMOTIONS AND THE BODY

Learning Objective: People communicate emotion through touch as well as through words. This exercise helps you become more aware and familiar with different emotions and assists with accurately identifying emotions through touch.

NOTE: This exercise is based on the research of Hertenstein, et al. at DePauw University. Their paper can be found at: http://www.gruberpeplab.com/teaching/psych3131_spring2015/documents/6.2_Hertenstein_2006_TouchEmotions.pdf.

Instructions:
1. Find a partner who is willing to help you with this exercise.

2. The emotions that participants were able to decode in the study referenced above through touch included: anger, fear, disgust, love, gratitude, and sympathy. Select one of these words you would like to practice.

3. Have your partner turn away from you.

4. Begin by communicating the emotion by touching their arm (wrist to elbow only).

5. Have your partner guess the emotion you are trying to convey.

6. If your partner is willing, have them choose an emotion and have them communicate the emotion by touching your arm.

7. Continue with 3-5 more emotions.

8. If you want to practice more difficult emotions to express through touch, you can refer to Appendix Two and choose one from the emotions list.

9. After completing the exercise, answer the Discovery Questions.

Discovery Questions:

WHAT EMOTIONS WERE THE EASIEST TO IDENTIFY AND WHY?

WHAT EMOTIONS WERE MORE DIFFICULT TO IDENTIFY AND WHY?

IF YOU OR YOUR PARTNER WERE NOT ABLE TO GUESS THE CORRECT EMOTION, WHAT COULD HAVE BEEN DONE DIFFERENTLY?

MAP EXERCISE 8:
COMMUNICATE THROUGH TOUCH

Learning Objective: Understanding the emotional tone or culture of an organization is an important part of being a more emotionally intelligent leader. Oftentimes, organizations and groups have unspoken display rules people must adhere to rather than showing their real emotions. Identifying and understanding display rules is important when fitting into the culture. This exercise will help you identify your organization's display rules and highlight dissonance between what is being displayed and what is being felt.

Instructions:

1. Think about an organization and/or group you belong to and reflect on what it feels like to be in your organization or group. How do people generally express and how often do people feel the emotions listed in the Workplace Emotions table?

2. Keeping your organization and/or group in mind, review the common emotions displayed and felt in a typical day.

3. Circle the frequency of emotions (1 – never, 3 – often, 5 - always) you see expressed and felt in your workplace for each emotion.

4. Upon completion, answer the Discovery Questions.

Workplace Emotions:

Emotion	Frequency Expressed	Frequency Felt
Happy - Gain something of value	1 · 2 · 3 · 4 · 5	1 · 2 · 3 · 4 · 5
Sad - Lose something of value	1 · 2 · 3 · 4 · 5	1 · 2 · 3 · 4 · 5
Surprise - Something unexpected happened	1 · 2 · 3 · 4 · 5	1 · 2 · 3 · 4 · 5
Anger - Blocked from getting something you want	1 · 2 · 3 · 4 · 5	1 · 2 · 3 · 4 · 5
Fear - Your well-being is in danger	1 · 2 · 3 · 4 · 5	1 · 2 · 3 · 4 · 5
Disgust - Your values are violated or offended	1 · 2 · 3 · 4 · 5	1 · 2 · 3 · 4 · 5
Pride - Achieving something important	1 · 2 · 3 · 4 · 5	1 · 2 · 3 · 4 · 5
Gratitude - Love and appreciation of something you value	1 · 2 · 3 · 4 · 5	1 · 2 · 3 · 4 · 5

Discovery Questions:

> WHAT EMOTIONS ARE EXPRESSED THE MOST AT YOUR ORGANIZATION AND WHY?

> WHAT EMOTIONS ARE FELT MOST AT YOUR ORGANIZATION AND WHY?

> WHAT IMPACT ARE THE DISPLAY RULES HAVING ON YOU AND YOUR ORGANIZATION?

WHICH EMOTIONS ARE MORE HIDDEN, MEANING THEY ARE FELT BUT NOT EXPRESSED AND WHY?

WHAT IS CAUSING THE DISSONANCE BETWEEN EMOTIONS EXPRESSED AND EMOTIONS FELT? WHAT DOES THIS INFORMATION PROVIDE ABOUT THE EMOTIONAL CULTURE OF YOUR ORGANIZATION AND/OR GROUP?

WHAT EMOTIONS WOULD BE MORE HELPFUL IN YOUR ORGANIZATION AND OR/GROUP IF THEY WERE EXPRESSED MORE FREQUENTLY AND WHY?

MAP EXERCISE 9: EXPRESSING EMOTIONS ACCURATELY

Learning Objective: We feel many emotions throughout the day and express each one differently. Therefore, being authentic with your emotions, and displaying them correctly, is important as it allows others to understand you better. This exercise helps you get better at displaying the correct emotion that matches the emotion you are feeling.

Instructions:

1. Use your smartphone or computer's video recording application.

2. Select an emotion word from Appendix Two, Emotion Word List.

3. Turn on the record function and express one of the emotions. Without words, begin with basic emotions such as happiness, anger, and sadness.

4. Review the video and see if you can clearly tell the emotion you were trying to display.

5. Once you master the basic emotions, try more complex emotions such as annoyed, frustrated, optimism, disgust, and love.

6. When you feel you mastered displaying the appropriate emotion, ask someone you trust if you could practice displaying the emotions and have them guess to see how well you did!

7. If you want to go a step further in developing your emotional accuracy, keep your camera on during video meetings and pay attention to whether the emotion you are displaying on camera matches the emotion you are feeling.

Discovery Questions:

WHAT EMOTION WAS THE EASIEST TO DISPLAY AND WHY?

WHAT EMOTION WAS THE HARDEST TO DISPLAY AND WHY?

WHEN PRACTICING THIS EXERCISE WITH ANOTHER PERSON, HOW ACCURATE WERE THEY IN GUESSING YOUR INTENDED EMOTION? WERE THERE EMOTIONS THAT WERE EASIER OR HARDER FOR THEM TO IDENTIFY? WHAT ADVICE OR FEEDBACK DID THEY PROVIDE TO HELP YOU DISPLAY THE EMOTION MORE ACCURATELY?

IF YOU PRACTICED WATCHING YOUR EMOTIONS DURING A VIDEO CONVERSATION, WHAT EMOTIONS, IF ANY, DID YOU CHOOSE TO SUPPRESS AND WHY?

HOW DOES SUPPRESSING EMOTIONS HELP OR HINDER PEOPLE FROM UNDERSTANDING HOW YOU ARE FEELING? WHAT IMPACT COULD SUPPRESSING EMOTIONS HAVE ON YOUR RELATIONSHIP WITH OTHERS?

MAP EXERCISE 10: "HOW ARE YOU?"

Learning Objective: The first ability of EI is to identify emotions and it is critical to do this accurately. One way to get important emotional "data" is by asking people "how are you?" in a way that elicits an honest response – which is not something too many people give! This exercise helps increase awareness of the accuracy of data you receive when trying to map someone's emotional state.

Instructions:

1. In the course of a day, observe how many times you ask someone "how are you?" or they ask you.

2. Note how long before you or the other person responds to the question, their response, tone of voice, and body language during the interaction.

3. Record the information after each exchange and at the end of the day, answer the Discovery Questions.

Discovery Questions:

WHAT WERE SOME OF THE MORE COMMON REPLIES FROM YOU?

WHAT WERE SOME OF THE MORE COMMON REPLIES FROM OTHERS?

HOW LONG DID IT TAKE YOU OR THE PERSON TO RESPOND TO THE QUESTION?

WHAT TONE OF VOICE DID EACH PERSON USE? WAS IT UPBEAT, NEUTRAL, OR UNPLEASANT? DID THE TONE MATCH THE WORDS, BODY LANGUAGE, AND FACIAL EXPRESSION?

DID ANYONE RESPOND WITH A MORE DETAILED RESPONSE AND HOW DID THE OTHER PERSON RESPOND IN RETURN?

WHAT DID YOU LEARN FROM THESE OBSERVATIONS? WHAT DATA ARE PEOPLE SENDING WHEN THEY RESPOND TO THE "HOW ARE YOU" QUESTION?

MAP EXERCISE 11:
OTHER WAYS TO GET EMOTIONAL DATA

Learning Objective: Getting good emotional data on others can be challenging. Not everyone is willing to respond or perhaps the organizational culture does not value this kind of information. Therefore, to get good emotional data, you must find ways to figure it out without asking the ubiquitous "How are you?". This exercise presents different ways to get emotional data from others who may be resistant, or do not readily share this kind of information.

Instructions:
1. Think of several people who do not share how they are feeling verbally and write them down in the table below.

2. For each person, consider their personality, social style, and anything else you know about this person's typical interactions with others. Record your observations for each person in the table. (For example, are they an extrovert, introvert, analytical, expressive, workaholic, joker, serious, etc.?)

3. After you record the person and how you observe them, approach each person and ask, "How are you?" in an authentic manner. Record their answers in the table under the Response heading.

4. If you received an authentic answer, meaning their words matched their facial expression, body language and they shared why they felt the way they did, congratulations! You must have asked "how are you?" in a way that invited a genuine answer. Mark yes, under the Authentic column. However, if you did not get an accurate response, enter "no", and answer the Discovery Questions. We included a "Maybe" response for you to consider the response more deeply – and to reflect on how you can obtain additional data to make a more informed decision.

Person	Obervable Behaviors	Response	Authentic
Example: David	*Serious, analytical, private, dry sense of humor*	*Great, awesome!*	○ Yes ● No ○ Maybe
			○ Yes ○ No ○ Maybe
			○ Yes ○ No ○ Maybe
			○ Yes ○ No ○ Maybe
			○ Yes ○ No ○ Maybe

Warning: If you are in a position of power or influence, asking "how are you?" of staff who traditionally do not have a voice leverages your power dynamic in an unfair manner. Start with colleagues and as you build trust, expand this exercise to include other people.

Discovery Questions:

DESCRIBE YOUR PERSONAL STYLE. ARE YOU MORE OF AN UPBEAT, HIGH-ENERGY PERSON OR LOW-KEY? HOW MIGHT YOUR STYLE IMPACT THE RESPONSE FROM THE OTHER PERSON?

HOW DID PEOPLE REACT TO YOU ASKING, "HOW ARE YOU"? DID THEY STOP AND ENGAGE? DID THEY IGNORE THE QUESTION? DID THEY GIVE THE STANDARD CANNED ANSWER OF "GOOD, GREAT, OR OK?"

WHAT, IF ANYTHING, DID YOU LEARN FROM THEIR RESPONSES?

IF YOU DID NOT GET AN AUTHENTIC ANSWER, WHAT OTHER QUESTIONS MIGHT YOU ASK NEXT TIME YOU SEE THIS PERSON INSTEAD OF "HOW ARE YOU"? (SOME IDEAS INCLUDE: HOW ARE THINGS? HOW ARE YOU FEELING ABOUT THIS PROJECT? WHAT DO YOU THINK ABOUT X? ON A SCALE OF 1 TO 10, HOW DO YOU FEEL ABOUT X?)

IF YOU STILL ARE NOT ABLE TO GET AN ANSWER ON HOW PEOPLE ARE FEELING, CONSIDER THE FOLLOWING QUESTIONS: HOW CAN YOU USE THE MOOD MAP TO GAUGE HOW PEOPLE ARE FEELING? HOW CAN YOU USE THEIR BODY LANGUAGE, TONE OF VOICE AND FACIAL EXPRESSIONS TO GAUGE HOW THEY ARE FEELING? HOW CAN YOU SHARE YOUR FEELINGS WITH OTHERS TO ROLE MODEL WHAT AN AUTHENTIC ANSWER LOOKS LIKE? JOT DOWN A FEW IDEAS ON HOW YOU WILL HANDLE THIS SITUATION NEXT TIME, IN THE SPACE BELOW.

SECOND ABILITY: MATCH EMOTION

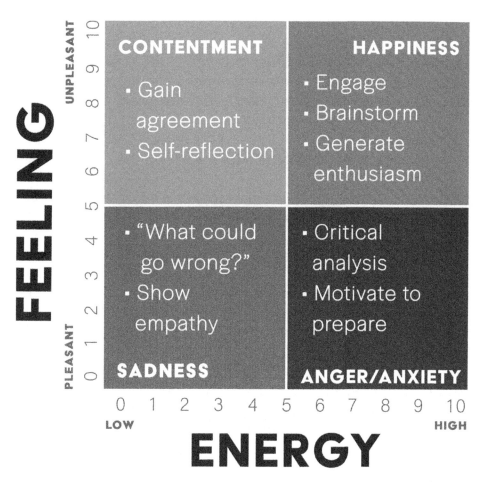

Now that you have practiced how to accurately Map emotions, the next ability is to determine if these emotions are helpful to the situation. As discussed previously, how we feel influences how we think and how we behave. Therefore, there are certain emotions that are better suited for accomplishing certain tasks. For example, if you are attending a celebratory event - joy and happiness would be a better emotion than frustration or boredom. The key is knowing which emotion is required for the task at hand and being able to generate those emotions in yourself and others. We can also use emotions to connect to others through empathy. When you feel what others feel, it creates a personal bond that builds trust.

The following exercises will help strengthen your ability to determine what emotions are more helpful in certain situations and how to generate these emotions in yourself and others.

MATCH EMOTION EXERCISE 1: FEELING EMOTIONS WITH STORYTELLING

· Group Activity ·

Learning Objective: When we feel an emotion, both our thinking and physical body changes. You may experience emotions when reading a book, hearing a story, listening to music or being in nature. This exercise helps us practice empathy – to feel what others feel – through storytelling. The goal is for the listener to feel the emotions being conveyed by the storyteller – to establish an emotional connection. The story can be fictional or true, but please be aware when sharing a story that evokes anger or sadness, the listener may continue to feel these emotions long after the story is over – so please use caution! We recommend sharing an inspirational or happy story when you are first practicing and then experiment with unpleasant emotions later.

Instructions:

1. Participants get into pairs with one being the storyteller and the other the listener.

2. The storyteller will have five minutes to share a story that has a strong emotional component. The listener simply listens without adding commentary.

3. The story can be real or fiction or can be someone else's story.

4. After the first person shares their story, complete the Discovery Questions below.

5. Repeat the above steps and reverse roles so the listener is now the storyteller and the storyteller is now the listener.

6. CRITICAL FINAL STEP: Sharing a story generates real feelings. If the last story generates anger or sadness, or any emotion on the Unpleasant scale, someone in the pair should tell a story reflecting an emotion high on the Pleasant scale.

Discovery Questions:

WHAT EMOTIONS WERE THE STORYTELLER TRYING TO CONVEY?

WHAT EMOTIONS DID THE LISTENER FEEL WHILE THE STORY WAS BEING TOLD?

IF THERE WAS A MATCH OF EMOTION BETWEEN THE STORYTELLER AND THE LISTENER, WHAT DID THE STORYTELLER DO TO EVOKE THE SAME EMOTIONS IN THE LISTENER?

IF THERE WAS NOT A MATCH, CONSIDER THESE QUESTIONS FOR THE MISMATCH

WHAT EMOTIONS MADE THE LISTENER FEEL UNCOMFORTABLE?

WHAT EMOTIONS DID THE STORYTELLER HAVE DIFFICULTY EMOTING?

WHAT WAS IT ABOUT THE SPECIFIC STORY CONTENT THAT WAS DIFFICULT TO FEEL?

WHAT WAS IT ABOUT THE WAY THE EMOTION WAS SHARED THAT MADE IT DIFFICULT TO FEEL?

WHAT WAS IT ABOUT HOW THE LISTENER PROCESSED THE STORY THAT MAY HAVE CONTRIBUTED TO THE MISMATCH?

IF THE LISTENER DID NOT FEEL THE EMOTIONS THE STORYTELLER WAS TRYING TO CONVEY, WHAT COULD THE STORYTELLER HAVE DONE DIFFERENTLY?

WHAT CAN BE LEARNED FROM THIS EXERCISE ABOUT THE IMPORTANCE OF STORYTELLING AND EMOTIONS?

WHAT STORY COULD YOU SHARE RIGHT NOW WITH YOUR TEAM TO GET THEM INTO THE RIGHT EMOTIONAL STATE TO COMPLETE THEIR TASKS?

ADVANCED EXERCISE: Each person selects an emotion from the Emotion Word List listed, in Appendix Two, at random. They then tell a story about a time they experienced that emotion. Due to the powerful nature of this exercise, people can either opt out or select a different emotion.

MATCH EMOTION EXERCISE 2:
HOW EMOTIONS IMPACT THINKING AND BEHAVIOR

• **Group or Individual Activity** •

Learning Objective: We know emotions influence our thinking and impact our behavior. This quick exercise demonstrates the link between emotions and thinking and how odd it feels when there is a disconnect between the two.

Instructions:

1. Ask the group to please stand up and explain the learning objective for the exercise. (Or simply follow these instructions if you are going through the Workbook on your own.)

2. Ask the group to tighten their entire body - fists, face, jaws, shoulders – and to squint their eyes, breathe quickly and lock their knees.

3. While they are in this tense state, ask them to quickly name something that makes them happy. (Chances are this may take a little while for them to respond or they may seem confused – this is to be expected.)

4. Now tell the group to relax their shoulders, move about the room and finally, take a big deep breath through their mouth, exhale and smile. This will help shift them into a state of contentment and relaxation.

Discovery Questions:

> HOW EASY OR HARD WAS IT TO SAY SOMETHING THAT MAKES YOU HAPPY? WHY DO YOU THINK IT WAS EASY OR HARD?

WHERE IN YOUR BODY DO YOU HOLD STRESS?

WHAT ACTION DO YOU TAKE TO NOTICE HOW YOU ARE FEELING?

WHAT ACTION DO YOU TAKE TO REDUCE STRESS?

CRITICAL NOTE: please do this exercise in this order, that is, the second round should generate more pleasant sensations.

MATCH EMOTION EXERCISE 3: GROUP BRAINSTORMING

· **Group Activity** ·

Learning Objective: Emotions are contagious, especially when in group settings. Therefore, it is important to set the right emotional tone when engaging others to ensure the emotions match the intended goal. This exercise demonstrates how a leader's emotions have a powerful impact on the group. Note: Select the team leaders ahead of time and allow them to decline. Explain the task (read the instructions several times) and ensure that the leaders can follow the instructions and are not feeling pressured to volunteer.

Instructions:
The instructions for this exercise can be found at: https://bit.ly/3pTWliq

Discovery Questions:

HOW DID EACH TEAM FEEL DURING THE PROCESS?

HOW DO YOU FEEL NOW THAT THE EXERCISE IS OVER?

HOW DID EACH TEAM WORK TOGETHER DURING THE PROCESS?

HOW DID THE LEADER IMPACT THE DISCUSSION?

HOW DID EACH TEAM DO WITH GENERATING IDEAS? WHO HAD THE MOST? LEAST? WHY?

DID ANY TEAM MEMBER TRY TO CHANGE THE MOOD OF THE DISCUSSION AND IF YES, DID IT WORK? WHY OR WHY NOT?

WHAT COULD HAVE BEEN DONE DIFFERENTLY DURING THE MEETING THAT WOULD HAVE RESULTED IN A BETTER OUTCOME?

HOW DO YOU SEE THESE SORTS OF MEETINGS PLAYING OUT IN YOUR ENVIRONMENT? WHAT COULD YOU DO TO MOVE A MEETING'S TONE IF IT IS HEADING IN THE WRONG DIRECTION?

MATCH EMOTION EXERCISE 4:
MATCHING EMOTIONS TO THE TASK AT HAND

Learning Objective: When attempting to reach goals and complete tasks, there are emotions that are better suited for the situation than others. Therefore, it is important to notice when your current emotions are not helping your intended goal and shift your emotion to a more helpful one. This exercise raises your awareness of your current emotions, what emotions are better for the situation and provides an opportunity to experiment with different strategies for moving your emotions to where they need to be.

Instructions:

1. For the next 5 days, keep the journal pages (below) with you.

2. When you are about to do an important task, list the task, the emotion you are currently feeling (Map) and the emotion that would be most helpful to accomplish the task (Match) in the table below.

3. To determine which strategy would work best in the situation, review the various Move strategies listed in this Workbook under MOVE EMOTION EXERCISE 6 and list it in the last column of the journal.

4. At the end of 5 days, answer the Discovery Questions.

MATCHING EMOTION TO THE TASK AT HAND JOURNAL

DAY	TASK	EMOTION FELT (MAP)	IDEAL EMOTION (MATCH)	STRATEGY TO SUSTAIN OR MOVE EMOTION
MONDAY				
TUESDAY				
WEDNESDAY				
THURSDAY				
FRIDAY				
SATURDAY				
SUNDAY				

Discovery Questions:

AFTER REVIEWING YOUR JOURNAL, WHAT DO YOU NOTICE ABOUT YOUR CURRENT EMOTIONS AND YOUR DESIRED EMOTIONS NECESSARY TO COMPLETE THE TASK?

WHAT PATTERNS DO YOU SEE BETWEEN THE CURRENT EMOTIONS AND THE DESIRED ONES? DO YOU TEND TO BE CONSISTENT OR INCONSISTENT WITH YOUR EMOTIONS FROM TASK TO TASK?

WHAT EMOTIONS DO YOU SEE REPEATING? ARE YOUR CURRENT EMOTIONS TYPICALLY THE ONES NEEDED IN THE SITUATION? WHY OR WHY NOT?

IF YOU WERE NOT IN THE CORRECT EMOTIONAL SPACE, WHAT STRATEGIES DID YOU USE TO GET YOURSELF IN THE MOST DESIRED EMOTIONAL PLACE? HOW EASY OR DIFFICULT WAS THIS TO DO?

WHAT WILL YOU DO TO BECOME MORE AWARE OF YOUR CURRENT EMOTIONS TO ENSURE YOU GENERATE THE RIGHT EMOTIONS FOR THE TASK AT HAND?

MATCH EMOTION EXERCISE 5:
LEVERAGING EMOTIONS FOR SUCCESSFUL OUTCOMES

Learning Objective: While it is important to recognize your emotions, it is equally important to recognize the emotions of a team. As a leader, you will have to take action to move a team's emotional tone to a more helpful one to achieve team goals. This exercise raises your awareness of group emotional dynamics and encourages practicing ways to shift the team's emotions to achieve better outcomes.

Instructions:

1. For the next 5 days, observe emotions displayed in group settings by completing the template below.

2. Each time you are in a group setting, whether it is on the phone, group e-mail or virtual, notice the emotions that are present (Map).

3. Once you identify the emotion, decide what action you will take to either sustain or move the team's emotions to a better emotional climate (Match/Move).

4. Notice what impact you had on the emotional tone or climate.

5. At the end of 5 days, answer the Discovery Questions.

Discovery Questions:

REVIEWING THE TEMPLATE, WHAT DO YOU NOTICE ABOUT THE EMOTIONS OF CERTAIN GROUPS? DID YOU NOTICE PATTERNS OF EMOTIONS OR DIVERGING EMOTIONS DEPENDING ON THE GROUP?

IF THE EMOTION WAS NOT IDEAL, WHAT ACTION DID YOU TAKE TO MOVE THE EMOTIONS TO A MORE HELPFUL ONE?

WHAT EMOTIONS DO YOU SEE REPEATING? IS YOUR GROUP'S EMOTIONAL CLIMATE TYPICALLY THE ONE NEEDED IN THE SITUATION? WHY OR WHY NOT?

IF YOUR GROUP WAS NOT DISPLAYING THE CORRECT EMOTIONAL TONE, WHAT STRATEGIES DID YOU USE TO GET THEM TO THE MORE DESIRABLE EMOTIONS? HOW EASY OR DIFFICULT WAS THIS TO DO?

WHAT WILL YOU DO TO BECOME MORE AWARE OF YOUR TEAM'S CURRENT EMOTIONAL TONE TO ENSURE YOU ARE IN THE RIGHT PLACE FOR THE TASK AT HAND BEFORE AND DURING INTERACTING WITH YOUR TEAM?

MATCHING EMOTION FOR SUCCESSFUL OUTCOMES

DAY	SETTING	PEOPLE INVOLVED	IDEAL EMOTION (MATCH)	YOUR ROLE
MONDAY				
TUESDAY				
WEDNESDAY				
THURSDAY				
FRIDAY				
SATURDAY				
SUNDAY				

MATCH EMOTION EXERCISE 6: PRACTICING EMPATHY

Learning Objective: Emotionally intelligent leaders put themselves in other people's shoes in an effort to feel what the other person is feeling, even when they have never had the same experience. This is called emotional empathy and plays an important role in building relationships and trust with others. This reflective exercise helps you practice empathy and how doing so will improve relationships with others.

Instructions:

1. During conversations with others, practice being truly present with that person.

2. To ensure you are practicing deep listening, eliminate distractions and focus not only on the words, but the emotions you are sensing as well.

3. Quiet your mind. Do not judge the other person, do not offer advice, simply listen.

4. If the person is sharing an emotional story, see if you can feel what the other person is conveying. Are they emoting joy, sadness, anger, frustration, boredom, etc.?

5. Once they have shared their story, offer gestures (nod your head, quiet smile of recognition, etc.) or words of kindness (I am sorry you experienced that) or support (Is there something I can help with?).

6. Notice how you both left the conversation and reflect on the Discovery Questions.

Discovery Questions:

> HOW DID YOU PRACTICE BEING PRESENT WITH THE OTHER PERSON? WHAT STRATEGIES DID YOU USE?

HOW DIFFICULT OR EASY WAS IT TO BE PRESENT WITH THE OTHER PERSON? WHY WAS IT DIFFICULT OR EASY?

WHAT EMOTIONS DID THE OTHER PERSON COMMUNICATE? WHAT WERE THE UNDERLYING EMOTION THEMES OF THE STORY?

HOW DID YOU FEEL DURING THE CONVERSATION? DID YOU GENERATE THESE ACTIVELY OR DID THEY ARISE WITHOUT EFFORT?

WERE THE EMOTIONS YOU BOTH FELT DIFFERENT OR THE SAME? IF THEY WERE DIFFERENT, WHY DO YOU THINK THEY WERE DIFFERENT?

AT THE END OF THE CONVERSATION, HOW DID YOU BOTH FEEL?

REFLECTING ON THE CONVERSATION, WHAT WOULD YOU HAVE DONE DIFFERENTLY (IF ANYTHING) TO FEEL MORE EMPATHY FOR THIS PERSON?

MATCH EMOTION EXERCISE 7: EMOTIONAL CLIMATE CHANGE

Learning Objective: Emotions can help you think more clearly, make better decisions, and achieve goals more easily. This applies not only to individuals, but groups as well. Sometimes the emotions of the group are not suited for the situation. This exercise helps you reflect on the best emotional climate for your group, team, or classroom and how to generate the right emotion to ensure a successful outcome.

Instructions:

1. Think of a discussion you will be having soon that may prove challenging due to the topic or people involved. In the table, indicate what emotions would be most conducive to getting things done in your group (whether a team, committee, class or organization).

2. Once you know what emotions you want to generate for the group, indicate in the table, what behaviors and actions will you engage in to generate those emotions? Some examples include:

- ☐ **Respect:** Verbalize appreciation when people provide ideas or opinions. Focus on their efforts, behaviors and their ideas.
- ☐ **Acceptance:** Thank the person, whether you agree or not. Indicate that their view or expressed feeling is theirs and they are entitled to it.
- ☐ **Trust:** During a conversation open up and share something about yourself, something you may not be completely comfortable sharing (at the same time, be aware that you may not engender trust and the other person may reveal what you share).
- ☐ **Attentiveness:** Put the phone down, ask the person to sit, make appropriate eye
- ☐ contact and paraphrase what the other person says.
- ☐ **Hope:** Acknowledge a difficult situation or a setback. And then, indicate your
- ☐ confidence in the team or individual's ability to effect positive change and solve the problem using a slightly positive but not too effusive style (which might have a slightly "off" quality after a setback).
- ☐ **Compassion:** At times, people fall into despair. Trauma, loss, failure, illness happens and the greatest gift you can give someone is to listen, show empathy and ask how you can help. This goes a long way in cultivating meaningful relationships.

3. Finally, select one of these emotions and engage in some of the behaviors. Try this with different groups and individuals on different occasions and answer the Discovery Questions.

Situation	People Involved	Optimal Emotion	My Behaviors

Discovery Questions:

LIST THE EMOTION YOU TRIED TO CREATE, THE BEHAVIORS YOU TRIED AND THE REACTION:

LOOKING BACK ON THE CONVERSATION, WHAT WORKED WELL AND WHY?

HOW EFFECTIVE WERE YOU AT CREATING THAT EMOTION IN YOURSELF AND THE OTHER PERSON (PEOPLE)?

REFLECTING ON THE OUTCOME OF THE MEETING, WHAT WILL YOU DO DIFFERENTLY NEXT TIME?

MATCH EMOTION EXERCISE 8: EMOTIONS-BASED STORYTELLING

Learning Objective: Emotionally intelligent leaders fully engage with their own emotions and those of others. How well you do this depends on your level of skill, but we can enhance this skill through emotion-based storytelling. In fact, all good stories have a good plot and character development, but great stories connect with us emotionally. This exercise helps develop your story-telling skills and your ability to use emotions to connect with others.

Instructions:

1. Refamiliarize yourself with the four Mood Map quadrants, the emotions reflected in each, and how these emotions feel physically.

2. Jot down which emotion you want to engage in for each quadrant. Perhaps pick a less intense version of an unpleasant emotion to start with, for example, frustration rather than anger.

4. Recall a time you felt the selected emotion. For example, educators may want to pick a time they felt the emotion in the classroom, or a leader when they felt the emotion dealing with their team.

5. Write down the elements of the story in the table below. As you know, good stories often have a conflict followed by a resolution or a highpoint followed by a positive result.

6. Tell the story to yourself. Record it, review it, and edit the story. Tell it again and go through a few iterations to get the story down to one to two minutes while still retaining its power to generate the emotion. When you finish, your story should capture the emotion you want others to feel.

7. Once you are pleased with the final product, try telling your story to a friend or colleague. Ask for their honest feedback on what emotion they felt while you were telling your story. Perhaps use a 10-point scale with 1 being they didn't feel the emotion at all to 10 being they felt the emotion throughout their body. If you didn't get a 10, ask them what you would need to do to reach a 10 and then try it!

8. Finally, do make sure when practicing an emotion touchpoint story that you end with a pleasant emotion – one in the green or yellow quadrant.

Mood Map Quadrant/ Emotion	Setting	People	Situation	Outcome
Example: Yellow/ Excitement	*Leadership team meeting*	*My boss and peers*	*We were worried about budget cuts impacting our exciting new product plan*	*Our boss announced there would be no cuts and we could pursue our new initiative*
RED				
BLUE				
GREEN				
YELLOW				

Discovery Questions:

> HOW EASY OR DIFFICULT WAS IT TO TELL A STORY USING EMOTIONS? WHAT MADE IT EASY OR DIFFICULT?

> WERE THERE CERTAIN EMOTIONS THAT WERE EASIER THAN OTHERS? WHAT WERE THEY AND WHY?

> HOW EASY OR DIFFICULT WAS IT TO TELL A STORY USING EMOTIONS? WHAT MADE IT EASY OR DIFFICULT?

> IF YOU TOLD THE STORY TO OTHERS, WHAT WAS THEIR REACTION? WHICH EMOTIONS DID THEY FEEL THE MOST? LEAST? WHAT FEEDBACK DID THEY GIVE YOU TO IMPROVE YOUR STORY? WHAT WILL YOU DO DIFFERENTLY BASED ON THEIR FEEDBACK?

THIRD ABILITY: MEANING OF EMOTION

When making decisions, leaders use many sources of data but often forget that emotions contain extremely valuable information critical to decision making. Great leaders understand how emotions influence behaviors, engagement, trust and creativity. Therefore, it is critical to consider emotions and their impact on achieving organizational goals. The first step is being able to accurately label emotions and how these emotions progress and blend to form more complex emotions. The ability to make meaning of emotions also allows us to do emotional affective forecasting, being able to predict how people might react emotionally in certain situations. This information is invaluable when working with others to achieve common goals and mitigate disruptive emotions.

The following exercises will help improve your ability to label emotions, understand how emotions may progress over time and how to prepare for emotions to make effective decisions.

MEANING OF EMOTION EXERCISE 1: EMOTIONS IN THE WORKPLACE

Learning Objective: Emotions flow throughout organizations and, therefore, it is important to learn how emotions impact work outcomes. This exercise helps you become more aware of emotions in the workplace, how they can help or hinder individual and group performance and how to be more intentional in setting the right emotional tone for reaching organizational goals.

Instructions and Discovery Questions:

LIST THE TOP THREE INDIVIDUAL WORK ACTIVITIES THAT GENERATE UNPLEASANT EMOTIONS IN YOU

ACTIVITY	UNPLEASANT EMOTION
1.	1.
2.	2.
3.	3.

WHY DO THE ACTIVITIES ABOVE GENERATE UNPLEASANT EMOTIONS IN YOU? HOW DOES FEELING UNPLEASANT ABOUT THESE WORK ACTIVITIES IMPACT YOUR WORK?

UNDERSTANDING WHY THESE ACTIVITIES EVOKE UNPLEASANT EMOTION IN YOU, HOW CAN YOU SUSTAIN THESE EMOTIONS IF THEY ARE HELPFUL? HOW CAN YOU HELP OTHERS UNDERSTAND THESE UNPLEASANT EMOTIONS ARE HELPFUL?"

LIST THE TOP THREE INDIVIDUAL WORK ACTIVITIES THAT GENERATE PLEASANT EMOTIONS IN YOU

ACTIVITY	**PLEASANT EMOTION**
1.	1.
2.	2.
3.	3.

WHY DO THE ACTIVITIES ABOVE GENERATE PLEASANT EMOTIONS IN YOU? HOW DOES FEELING PLEASANT ABOUT THESE WORK ACTIVITIES IMPACT YOUR WORK?

UNDERSTANDING WHY THESE ACTIVITIES EVOKE POSITIVE EMOTIONS IN YOU, WHAT CAN YOU DO TO BRING THESE FEELINGS TO ALL YOUR WORK?

LIST THE TOP THREE WORK ACTIVITIES YOU PERFORM WITH A GROUP? WHAT EMOTIONS ARE YOU CURRENTLY EXPERIENCING? WHAT EMOTION WOULD BE IDEAL TO PERFORM THIS WORK MORE SUCCESSFULLY?

Activity	Current Emotion	Ideal Emotion

WHAT IS THE DISCONNECT BETWEEN THE CURRENT AND IDEAL EMOTION? WHAT ACTIONS WILL YOU TAKE TO TRANSITION YOUR GROUP'S EMOTION TO A MORE HELPFUL EMOTIONAL PLACE?

MEANING OF EMOTION EXERCISE 2: DIFFERENT EMOTIONAL CAUSES IN YOU AND OTHERS

Learning Objective: Emotions have basic, universal causes. However, each person has unique or specific reasons for their emotions, which may or may not be the same reason why we feel certain emotions. Therefore, it is important to understand the cause of emotion (Meaning) in others to predict how they might behave or think depending on their emotional state. This exercise helps you practice getting to understand others more deeply and what makes someone "tick."

Instructions:

1. Using the template below, consider each emotion and indicate what brings about each emotion in you.

2. Next, consider a person that is important to you professionally. What makes this person feel each of these emotions?

3. After completing the template, answer the Discovery Questions.

EMOTION	CAUSE	YOU	OTHER
FRUSTRATION	Blocked from something wanted or valued		
DISGUST	Values are violated		
HAPPINESS	Gain something of value		
WORRY	Possible threat		
SURPRISE	Something unexpected		
SADNESS	Lose something of value		

Discovery Questions:

> HOW EASY OR DIFFICULT WAS THE TEMPLATE TO FILL OUT FOR YOU? WHAT MADE IT EASY OR DIFFICULT TO COMPLETE?

> IF YOU FOUND COMPLETING THE TEMPLATE DIFFICULT, WHY DO YOU THINK THAT IS? WHAT CAN YOU DO TO BE MORE IN TOUCH WITH WHAT CAUSES YOU TO FEEL THESE EMOTIONS?

> HOW EASY OR DIFFICULT WAS THE TEMPLATE TO FILL OUT FOR THE OTHER PERSON? WHAT MADE IT EASY OR DIFFICULT TO COMPLETE?

IF YOU FOUND THE TEMPLATE DIFFICULT TO COMPLETE FOR THE OTHER PERSON, WHY DO YOU THINK THAT IS? WHAT CAN YOU DO TO BE MORE IN TOUCH WITH WHAT CAUSES THEM TO FEEL THESE EMOTIONS?

AS YOU REFLECT ON WHAT CAUSES THIS PERSON TO FEEL THE WAY THEY DO, HOW CAN YOU USE THIS INFORMATION TO IMPROVE YOUR RELATIONSHIP WITH THEM? HOW CAN YOU USE THIS INFORMATION TO BETTER PREDICT HOW THIS PERSON MIGHT REACT TO VARIOUS EVENTS OR SITUATIONS?

MEANING OF EMOTION EXERCISE 3: MEANING OF EMOTIONS THROUGH WHAT IF?

Learning Objective: Oftentimes, successful interactions with others depend on how we approach the individual, what we say, and how we say it. Therefore, it is important to understand how emotions play a key role in conversations. This exercise will help you prepare for critical interactions by using a "What If" scenario (sometimes referred to as "affective emotional forecasting").

Instructions:

1. Before your next important interaction with your boss, co-worker, or colleague, take time to answer the Discovery Questions.

2. When answering the questions, it helps to be feeling pleasant or at least neutral. Make every attempt to be neutral, objective, and candid about the situation and what could happen.

3. If you are feeling unpleasant emotions, or do not feel you are being objective, ask someone you trust to provide you with feedback on your responses.

4. Once you feel emotionally prepared, you are now ready to engage with the other person(s).

5. After the interaction, review your responses to the Discovery Questions and compare them to what actually happened. If it went as planned, congratulations! And, if not, know things don't always turn out as planned and use this information to make improvements for your next interaction.

Discovery Questions:

WHAT IS THE PURPOSE OF THE MEETING?

WHAT DO I WANT THE OUTCOME TO BE AFTER THE DISCUSSION?

WHO IS INVOLVED IN THE MEETING?

WHAT IS THE OVERALL MOOD OR EMOTION OF THE PERSON(S) INVOLVED AND HOW MIGHT THEIR FEELINGS IMPACT THEIR BEHAVIOR DURING THE MEETING?

WHERE IS THE BEST PLACE AND TIME TO HAVE THE DISCUSSION?

KNOWING THE PERSON(S) INVOLVED, HOW SHOULD YOU PRESENT YOUR INFORMATION (TONE OF VOICE, MANNERISMS, TYPE OF PRESENTATION, ETC.)?

HOW MIGHT THE PERSON(S) REACT TO YOUR PROPOSAL/IDEA/REQUEST?

IF THE PERSON(S) REACTS NEGATIVELY (DEFENSIVELY) HOW WILL YOU CHOOSE TO REACT? WHAT STRATEGIES WILL YOU USE TO CONTINUE THE DIALOGUE IN A CONSTRUCTIVE MANNER?

HOW WILL YOU RESTATE THE INFORMATION IN A DIFFERENT WAY THAT MIGHT HELP THE PERSON(S) BECOME MORE RECEPTIVE TO THE CONVERSATION?

HOW WILL YOU END THE MEETING? WHAT WILL YOU SAY AND HOW WILL YOU ACT?

MEANING OF EMOTION EXERCISE 4: MAKING SENSE OF EMOTIONS
• Group and Individual Activity •

Learning Objective: Emotionally intelligent leaders understand how emotions progress from a mild state to an extreme state (for example, annoyance>anger>rage or acceptance>trust>adoration). Having a solid grasp on how emotions progress helps us better understand how a person will react and behave in certain situations. This exercise strengthens the ability to understand the nuances of emotions, how they change due to circumstances and to be better able to predict what might happen in certain situations.

Group Instructions:

1. Form groups of 4 to 6 people each.

2. Each group gets a deck of Emotions Flashcards (available at www.picturemypicture.com).

3. Place the flashcards face down on the table.

4. Each person selects 1 flashcard and views the card (but does not share with others).

5. The first person places their flashcard face up. The person begins to tell a story and uses the emotion listed on the flashcard in their story (two to five sentences).

6. The next person puts their flashcard face up and continues the same story, indicating what happens next that brings about this new emotion.

7. The remaining people continue the story, using their emotion in the story, until everyone has gone.

8. Typically, the story does not flow well because the emotions are random. As a team, rearrange the flashcards and as a group, re-tell the story that makes the most emotional sense.

9. As a team, answer the Discovery Questions.

Individual Instructions:

1. Place the flashcards face down on the table.

2. Select 6 flashcards and lay them face up in the order you chose them.

3. Now, recall a personal or work event that happened recently.

4. Begin recounting the event using each emotion in the order you picked them until all emotions are included in the story. Typically, the story does not flow well because the emotions are random.

5. Next, rearrange the flashcards in a way that makes the most emotional sense and retell the story. Hopefully, it will make a lot more sense!

6. Once you complete the exercise, answer the Discovery Questions.

Discovery Questions:

> HOW DIFFICULT OR EASY WAS THE FIRST PART OF THE EXERCISE WITHOUT A LOGICAL ORDER OF THE EMOTIONS? WHAT MADE IT DIFFICULT OR EASY?

> WHAT DID YOU NOTICE ABOUT YOUR OWN OR OTHERS' EMOTIONS DURING THE FIRST ROUND OF STORYTELLING?

> HOW DIFFICULT OR EASY WAS IT TO PUT THE EMOTIONS IN LOGICAL ORDER DURING THE SECOND ROUND OF STORYTELLING? WHAT MADE IT DIFFICULT OR EASY?

> NOW THAT YOU UNDERSTAND HOW EMOTIONS PROGRESS AND CHANGE, HOW CAN YOU USE THIS INFORMATION IN THE FUTURE?

MEANING OF EMOTION EXERCISE 5: INCREASING EMOTIONAL LITERACY

Learning Objective: Emotions have causes, and they also have patterns. The Emotion Wheel on this page provides a helpful way of viewing emotions. Emotion terms listed at the top of each hexagon are the most intense expression of the emotion, and the terms at the bottom are the least intense. This exercise helps you learn the "families" of emotions, understand the differences between emotions, and increases your emotional vocabulary to label emotions more succinctly.

Instructions:

1. Take a moment to review the Emotion Wheel to become familiar with the "families" of emotions and how they progress from less intense, to more intense emotions.

2. Think about the emotion words you express during a typical day. Look at your emails, memos, meetings, conversations, etc. and list the top 5 emotions you use in the first column of the table.

3. Reviewing the Emotion Word List in Appendix Two or the Emotion Families in Appendix Three, list the emotion that would be more appropriate for the situation.

4. After completing the table, answer the Discovery Questions.

Emotion Word Used Most Frequently	More Accurate Emotion Word
1.	
2.	
3.	
4.	
5.	

Discovery Questions:

OUT OF THE 5 EMOTION WORDS YOU USE FREQUENTLY, WHICH ONE DO YOU USE MOST FREQUENTLY AND WHY?

WHAT EMOTION WORDS DO YOU RARELY USE AND WHY?

WHAT EMOTION WORDS WOULD YOU LIKE TO USE MORE FREQUENTLY AND WHY?

LOOKING AT THE LIST OF MORE ACCURATE EMOTION WORDS YOU CHOSE, WHAT IMPACT DO YOU FEEL USING THESE WORDS WILL HAVE ON YOUR COMMUNICATION WITH OTHERS?

WHAT ACTION WILL YOU TAKE TO USE MORE ACCURATE EMOTION WORDS GOING FORWARD?

MEANING OF EMOTION EXERCISE 6: IMPROVING COMMUNICATION

Learning Objective: People feel numerous emotions throughout the day or week but may not accurately label how they feel. Being able to accurately label emotions provides others with data that helps them understand us better. This exercise helps you practice conveying the appropriate emotion when communicating with others.

Instructions:

1. Think of several upcoming communications you need to have at work.

2. In the first column of the table, list what type of communication (i.e., verbal, email, memo, phone call, etc.)

3. In the next column list who will be the recipient of your communication (i.e., colleague, employee, supervisor, etc.)

4. Review the Emotion Wheel and the Emotion Word List in Appendix Two and in the last column, list all the emotion words you would like to convey in your communication.

5. In the practice space below, draft your communication(s) using the emotion words you selected. Do more than one if you want more practice!

6. After you complete drafting your communication, answer the Discovery Questions.

Communication Method	Audience	Emotions to Convey

Discovery Questions:

WHEN COMMUNICATING WITH OTHERS, HOW OFTEN DO YOU USE EMOTION WORDS IN YOUR MESSAGING? WHY OR WHY NOT?

WHAT EMOTION WORDS DO YOU WANT TO CONVEY **MOST** OFTEN AND WHY?

WHAT EMOTION WORDS DO YOU WANT TO CONVEY **LEAST** OFTEN AND WHY?

AFTER WRITING YOUR PRACTICE COMMUNICATION USING THE EMOTION WORDS YOU WANT TO CONVEY, HOW DID YOU FEEL AFTER READING WHAT YOU WROTE? HOW DO THINK OTHERS WILL FEEL AFTER READING WHAT YOU WROTE?

WHAT WILL YOU DO DIFFERENTLY IN YOUR COMMUNICATION BECAUSE OF THIS EXERCISE?

MEANING OF EMOTION EXERCISE 7: MOOD OR EMOTION

Learning Objective: We are told emotions are data, but feelings are not always facts. Therefore, trusting your gut could result in making terrible decisions! That gut feel could be due to a mood rather than an emotion and moods are not reliable sources of information. This exercise helps you discover how decisions based on moods may lead to bad decisions.

Instructions:

1. Think about a recent time when you had a "bad feeling" about a decision. Describe the decision in the first column.

2. Next, list any emotions you were feeling associated with the decision. If other people were involved in the decision, include their feelings as well.

3. Consider the possible sources of the bad feeling which could include lack of sleep, hunger, a recent unrelated argument, world events, illness, not enough or too much caffeine, physical aches and pains, headache, bad weather, excessive traffic, etc. and list all sources that may have caused your mood.

4. On a scale from 0% to 100% consider to what extent the bad feeling was due to a mood.

5. After determining how much the decision was made due to mood, answer the Discovery Questions to analyze the situation further.

Decision	Associated Feelings	Emotions to Convey	% Mood

Discovery Questions:

> BEFORE MAKING THE "BAD" DECISION, WHAT DATA DID YOU USE TO MAKE THE DECISION?

> BASED ON YOUR ANALYSIS OF THE SITUATION, HOW DID THE SOURCE OF YOUR FEELINGS (AND THOSE OF OTHERS), IMPACT YOUR DECISION?

> HOW WILL THIS EXERCISE BETTER PREPARE YOU WHEN MAKING IMPORTANT DECISIONS?

FOURTH ABILITY: MOVE EMOTIONS

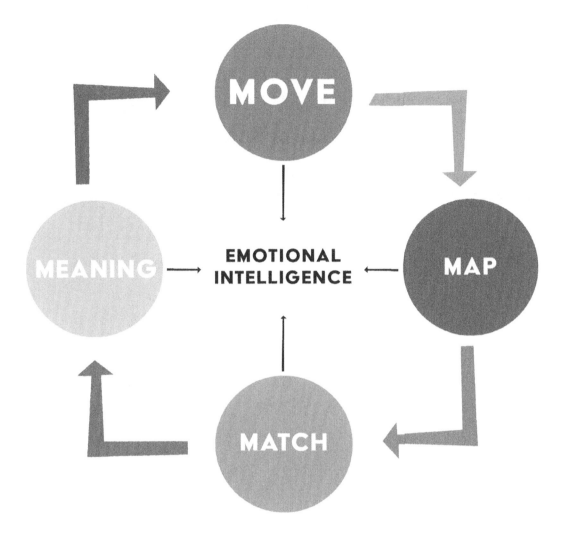

The fourth ability is the ability to Move (or sustain) your emotion and those of others. As you know, there are no "good" or "bad" emotions. The key is being able to match the emotions to the task or person and express emotions intelligently. The option of ignoring, avoiding, or suppressing emotions often leads to poor decision-making. The key is to notice emotions, stay open to them, and remain curious rather than judging them. The following Move exercises will develop your effective emotion management strategies, for yourself and others, and help you reach your desired goals and outcomes.

MOVE EMOTION EXERCISE 1: INEFFECTIVE STRATEGIES AUDIT

Learning Objective: Emotion management is critical to effective leadership. However, sometimes we lean on strategies that avoid addressing the underlying issue. While this may work short-term, they eventually become ineffective resulting in lack of trust, hard feelings, and broken relationships. This exercise helps you avoid short-term strategy pitfalls and deploy more effective Move strategies.

Instructions:

1. Take a moment to read each ineffective move strategy in the table.

2. In the second column, indicate which ones you typically use and how often.

3. After completing this workbook, return to this exercise and list some alternatives of how you can deploy more effective strategies.

4. After completing the table, answer the Discovery Questions.

INEFFECTIVE MOVE STRATEGY	USE/FREQUENCY	MY REPLACEMENT STRATEGY
BLAME OTHERS WITH HARSH CRITICISM WITHOUT SOLVING ISSUE	O FREQUENTLY O SOMETIMES O NEVER	
BLAME YOURSELF USING HARSH SELF-CRITICISM WITHOUT ADDRESSING ISSUE	O FREQUENTLY O SOMETIMES O NEVER	
PROCRASTINATE BY PUTTING THINGS OFF AND FREQUENT RESCHEDULING	O FREQUENTLY O SOMETIMES O NEVER	
AVOID ISSUE OR AVOID THE PERSON OR CONVERSATION	O FREQUENTLY O SOMETIMES O NEVER	
WISHFUL THINKING BY HOPING THINGS WILL GET BETTER WITHOUT ACTION	O FREQUENTLY O SOMETIMES O NEVER	
RUMINATE BY CONSTANTLY RE-HASHING THE EVENT OR EMOTION.	O FREQUENTLY O SOMETIMES O NEVER	
SUPPRESS EMOTIONS TO ALWAYS SHOW CONTROL	O FREQUENTLY O SOMETIMES O NEVER	
DENY AND CLAIM THERE IS NO PROBLEM	O FREQUENTLY O SOMETIMES O NEVER	
DAYDREAM TO AVOID DEALING WITH EMOTIONAL ISSUES	O FREQUENTLY O SOMETIMES O NEVER	
ABUSE DRUGS AND ALCOHOL TO AVOID DEALING WITH THE SITUATION	O FREQUENTLY O SOMETIMES O NEVER	
BEING AGGRESSIVE WITH OTHERS BY BULLYING OR LASHING OUT	O FREQUENTLY O SOMETIMES O NEVER	

Discovery Questions:

> WHICH INEFFECTIVE STRATEGIES DO YOU USE MOST OFTEN? WHY?

> WHAT IMPACT IS USING THESE INEFFECTIVE STRATEGIES HAVING ON YOU AND OTHERS?

> WHAT IDEAS DO YOU HAVE FOR REDUCING HOW OFTEN YOU USE INEFFECTIVE STRATEGIES?

> AFTER COMPLETING THE REMAINING MOVE EMOTION EXERCISES, WHICH EFFECTIVE MOVE STRATEGIES CAN YOU SWAP FOR THE INEFFECTIVE STRATEGIES YOU MOST OFTEN USE?

MOVE EMOTION EXERCISE 2:
FILLING UP YOUR EMOTIONAL RESERVE - GROUP

• **Group and Individual Activity** •

Learning Objective: We live in a constantly changing world that requires leaders to be at their best. Unfortunately, we tend to focus on the well-being of others and forget about our own well-being. This exercise helps a group or team get in touch with activities that rejuvenate, re-energize, and relax, and are enjoyable.

Instructions:

1. Take a moment, to list all the activities you like to do, that when you do them, you feel present, creative, productive, and happy. Enter your activities in the "Filling Up Your Emotional Reserve" space below.

2. Have each person in their group share their favorite activity.

3. Debrief the exercise by answering the Discovery Questions.

Discovery Questions:

FILLING UP YOUR EMOTIONAL RESERVE ACTIVITIES

Discovery Questions:

WHAT ABOUT THIS EXERCISE WAS DIFFICULT OR EASY? WHY?

HOW DID YOU FEEL DURING THE EXERCISE? WHY?

AS EVERYONE SHARED THEIR LIST, WHAT HAPPENED TO YOUR FEELINGS? OTHERS?

HOW DID YOU FEEL WHEN YOU SHARED YOUR LIST WITH OTHERS?

WHAT DID YOU LEARN FROM THIS EXERCISE THAT YOU CAN APPLY AT WORK?

MOVE EMOTION EXERCISE 3:
FILLING UP YOUR EMOTIONAL RESERVE - INDIVIDUAL

Learning Objective: We live in a VUCA (volatile, uncertain, complex, and ambiguous) environment that, at times, can be overwhelming, cause stress, and decrease productivity. This exercise helps you reflect on things you can do to strengthen your emotional resiliency and how to embed them into your daily life.

Instructions:

1. Take a moment, to list all the activities you like to do, that when you do them, you feel present, creative, productive, and happy. Enter your activities in the "Fill Up Your Emotional Reserve" space below.

2. Before continuing to step 3, answer the Discovery Questions.

3. During the upcoming week, choose at least one "flow" activity each day and list them below. If you cannot fully commit to an activity, modify it to meet your needs. For example, if exercise is something you enjoy, but you cannot fit it in due to time constraints, commit to taking the stairs, parking the car further from your office, or getting out at an earlier bus/metro stop.

Day	
MONDAY	
TUESDAY	
WEDNESDAY	
THURSDAY	
FRIDAY	
SATURDAY	
SUNDAY	

4. After completing a full week of filling up your emotional reserve, use the Reflection Journal space at the end of the exercise (or use your own journal), to reflect what you experienced during the week. What did you notice about yourself, your relationship with others, your overall mood? Feel free to reflect daily or at the end of the week.

FILLING UP YOUR EMOTIONAL RESERVE:

FILLING UP YOUR EMOTIONAL RESERVE:

Discovery Questions:

WHEN LISTING YOUR "FLOW" ACTIVITIES, HOW DIFFICULT OR EASY WAS IT FOR YOU TO COME UP WITH YOUR LIST? WHY DO YOU THINK IT WAS EASY OR HARD?

WHEN REVIEWING YOUR ACTIVITIES, WHICH ARE THE ONES YOU DO MOST FREQUENTLY, AND WHICH DO YOU DO INFREQUENTLY AND WHY?

LOOKING AT THE ACTIVITIES YOU ENJOY AND DO INFREQUENTLY, WHAT ACTION CAN YOU DO TO INTEGRATE THEM MORE INTO YOUR DAILY LIFE?

Please return to Instruction 3 to complete the exercise.

REFLECTION JOURNAL

MOVE EMOTION EXERCISE 4: PRACTICING MINDFULNESS

Learning Objective: Research shows how mindfulness helps clear the mind, rejuvenates the body, and open people to new possibilities. This exercise helps ground and center you, so you are ready to tackle the many challenges you face every day.

Instructions:

1. Find a place that is quiet, where you can be alone.

2. Remove all distractions such as phones, televisions, and computers.

3. Ensure your clothing feels comfortable.

4. Sit comfortably in a chair with your back firmly against the back of your chair and your feet securely on the ground.

5. Begin breathing normally at first, and then deepen and slow your breathing.

6. Take a deep breath in for the count of 4 and let it out completely as you silently count to 4 with your mouth closed. Just concentrate on counting and breathing. Do this for a few minutes.

7. Start your practice, by engaging all your senses. Open your eyes, if they were closed, and look around you. What do you see? Observe the colors, clarity, and depth of your surroundings.

8. Now, close your eyes and listen to the sounds around you. What do you hear in the foreground, in the background, and around you?

9. Shift your focus to smell. What are you smelling right now? Perhaps it is your coffee, your diffuser, your skin, your soap, etc. Do this for a few minutes.

10. Next, notice your skin and sense of touch. What is your skin touching – your clothes, chair, surface? Notice the touch of air on your skin.

11. Now that all senses are engaged, go back to step 6, inhaling and exhaling to the count of 4. Continue doing this for several minutes.

12. If your mind wanders, do not worry, this is normal. Just notice your mind is active and let it go like a balloon floating up in the air.

13. Once you feel grounded and ready to go back into the world, do so slowly. Take a moment to stretch, let out a big sigh and shake out the cobwebs. Hopefully, you feel better and ready to face the world!

14. When you are ready to reengage, take a moment to answer the Discovery Questions.

Discovery Questions:

> HOW DID YOU FIND PRACTICING MINDFULNESS? WAS IT EASY TO DO OR CHALLENGING? WHAT MADE IT EASY OR CHALLENGING? WHAT DID YOU NOTICE DURING YOUR PRACTICE?

> WHAT DID YOU NOTICE ABOUT YOURSELF AFTER ENGAGING IN THIS EXERCISE? HOW DID IT CHANGE THE WAY YOU FEEL? WHAT DID YOU NOTICE ABOUT HOW YOUR THOUGHTS OR INTERACTIONS WITH OTHERS AFTER PRACTICING?

> IN WHAT WAYS WILL YOU INCORPORATE MINDFULNESS INTO YOUR DAILY ACTIVITIES? WHAT SUPPORT DO YOU NEED TO CONTINUE THIS PRACTICE? HOW DO YOU THINK PRACTICING MINDFULNESS WILL CHANGE HOW YOU LEAD?

MOVE EMOTION EXERCISE 5: INTERVENING MOMENT

Learning Objective: There will be times when someone says or does something that causes an immediate and strong emotional reaction. Unfortunately, it is at these times we may say or do something we regret. While emotions are data, sometimes we get faulty data and react in a way we wish we had not. This exercise helps you insert an Intervening Moment to pause and reflect before acting.

Instructions:

1. Review each example of an Intervening Moment strategy.

2. List situations where you may have a reaction and say or do something you later regret.

3. Indicate which intervening action would be most appropriate for the situation (there may be more than one!).

4. Next, write down how you can specifically deploy the strategy and make it your own. These actions will only work if you practice them, plan for their use, and personalize them in a way you can use later in real-time.

INTERVENING MOMENT STRATEGY	SITUATION TO USE	MY SPECIFIC ACTION TO TAKE
EXAMPLE: **BREATHE -** Take a deep breath or two	*On a difficult phone call*	*When I sense I am getting defensive, go on mute, take a very deep breath, and return to the call.*
BREATHE - take a deep breath or two		
COUNT - slowly to 3		
REFLECT - Look down for a moment and reflect on what you are going to say		
PAUSE - and verbalize E.G. "Let me think about that"		
DRAFT - an email/ text but do not send it		
TAKE A BREAK - call for a break during a meeting		
INQUIRE - "Tell me more" to confirm other's meaning		

Discovery Questions:

> WHICH INTERVENING ACTIONS DID YOU USE AND HOW EFFECTIVE WERE THEY?

> IF YOU WERE UNABLE TO SUCCESSFULLY DEPLOY THESE STRATEGIES, WHAT HAPPENED?

> WHAT CAN YOU DO TO ENGAGE IN THESE STRATEGIES MORE FREQUENTLY AND EFFECTIVELY?

> IN WHAT OTHER WAYS CAN YOU STOP, PAUSE, AND REFLECT BEFORE RESPONDING?

MOVE EMOTION EXERCISE 6: MANAGING YOUR EMOTIONS

Learning Objective: There are times when how we feel is not the best emotion for the situation. Therefore, learning how to move emotions in real time is critical to successful leadership. This exercise familiarizes you with different Move strategies that can help you reach desired outcomes and goals.

Instructions:

1. Think of situations where unhelpful emotions might occur (i.e., during a phone call, conducting employee appraisal, leading a meeting, working on an important project, etc.).

2. Review the Move strategies below and select the best strategy for the situation.

3. Enter the situation in the second column.

4. In the last column, list as many specific actions you will take to deploy your chosen strategy.

5. After completing the table, answer the Discovery Questions.

MOVE STRATEGY	SITUATION	MY MOVE ACTIONS
Prepare for what might happen during interactions		
Modify your mood to psych yourself up or calm yourself down		
Reappraise the situation to see if there is another way of viewing it		
Deploy **Self-talk** and use your inner voice to calm or motivate		
Use **Physiological** methods, such as deep breathing, stretching, or smiling		
Express a different emotion using your voice, words, tone and posture		

Discovery Questions:

WHAT MOVE STRATEGIES DID YOU TRY AND HOW EFFECTIVE WERE THEY?

WHAT WAS CHALLENGING AND HOW CAN YOU MODIFY YOUR MOVE ACTIONS TO BE MORE EFFECTIVE?

WHAT STRATEGIES WERE THE MOST DIFFICULT TO DEPLOY? WHY?

WHAT STRATEGIES ARE THE EASIEST FOR YOU? WHY?

WHAT OTHER ACTIONS CAN YOU TAKE TO MOVE YOUR EMOTIONS GOING FORWARD?

MOVE EMOTION EXERCISE 7:
MANAGING YOUR EMOTIONS WITH LONG TERM STRATEGIES

Learning Objective: Leaders are judged on how they comport themselves and under stress, managing emotions becomes even more challenging. This exercise helps you take action to integrate long term emotional management strategies into your daily routine.

Instructions:

1. Take a moment to read each long term move strategy and example listed in the first two columns in the table.

2. Under "My Action Plan" list what actions you will do to deploy these beneficial long-term strategies.

3. After following your action plan for a week, answer the Discovery Questions.

STRATEGY	MY ACTION PLAN
EXAMPLE: *Diet and Nutrition: substitute healthier option; track what you eat*	*Switch location of our weekly management lunch to a place with a healthy salad bar*
DIET AND NUTRITION - substitute what you eat for a healthier option	
EXCERCISE - skip the elevator, take the stairs	
MEDITATION - practice mindfulness and meditation	
PRAYER - participate in religious practices and affiliation	
SLEEP - use a white noise machine to disconnect, learn a relaxation technique	
HOBBY - attend a cooking class, learn a new language or how to play an instrument	
TIME OFF - take your vacation days, enter them into your calendar	

Discovery Questions:

> WHICH STRATEGIES DID YOU ATTEMPT AND WHAT IMPACT DID THEY HAVE ON YOUR EMOTIONAL WELL-BEING?

> WHAT WAS THE EASIEST STRATEGY TO DEPLOY? WHY?

> WHAT WAS THE HARDEST STRATEGY TO DEPLOY? WHY?

> BASED ON THIS LIST AND YOUR LIFESTYLE, WHAT OTHER STRATEGIES MIGHT BE EFFECTIVE FOR YOU?

MOVE EMOTION EXERCISE 8: EMOTIONAL CONNECTIONS AT WORK

Learning Objective: The previous exercise listed long-term strategies for managing emotions. We purposely did not include the strategy, emotional connection in the exercise, and because it is so important, we made it a separate exercise. The social bonds of family, friends, and colleagues are vital to long-term emotional health. This exercise focuses on how to build strong emotional connections with people at work.

Instructions:

1. Take a moment to read each long term move strategy and example listed in the first two columns in the table.

2. Under "My Action Plan" list what actions you will do to deploy these beneficial long-term strategies.

3. After following your action plan for a week, answer the Discovery Questions.

PERSON	STATUS	NOTES	ACTION
EXAMPLE: Deborah	O CURRENT ● RECONNECT O ESTABLISH	She transferred to a new office and I am sad we no longer hang out	I will schedule to meet for coffee halfway between offices every 2 weeks or so
	O CURRENT O RECONNECT O ESTABLISH		
	O CURRENT O RECONNECT O ESTABLISH		
	O CURRENT O RECONNECT O ESTABLISH		
	O CURRENT O RECONNECT O ESTABLISH		
	O CURRENT O RECONNECT O ESTABLISH		
	O CURRENT O RECONNECT O ESTABLISH		

Discovery Questions:

> LOOKING BACK ON THE WEEK, HOW DID IT FEEL ESTABLISHING AN EMOTIONAL CONNECTION WITH YOUR COLLEAGUES?

> WERE THERE PEOPLE WHO IT WAS EASIER OR MORE DIFFICULT TO CONNECT WITH? WHY?

> WHAT WERE YOUR COLLEAGUE'S REACTION TO YOU REACHING OUT TO THEM TO CONNECT?

WHAT IMPACT DO YOU THINK CONNECTING TO YOUR COLLEAGUES WILL HAVE ON YOUR INDIVIDUAL AND TEAM WORK?

HOW CAN YOU CREATE AND MAINTAIN HEALTHY WORK RELATIONSHIPS WITH YOUR COLLEAGUES GOING FORWARD?

GO BACK TO MEANING EXERCISE 2. HOW CAN YOU USE THIS EXERCISE TO HELP YOU STRENGTHEN EXISTING RELATIONSHIPS AND CREATE NEW ONES?

MOVE EMOTION EXERCISE 9: MANAGING OTHERS' EMOTIONS

Learning Objective: Learning how to manage and move emotions is critical to successful leadership. At times you will have to manage your own emotions, as well as those of others. This exercise helps you learn the different strategies for managing others' emotions and creates an action plan to help your team achieve their goals.

Instructions:
1. Think of situations where unhelpful emotions might occur when interacting with others (i.e., during a phone call, conducting employee appraisals, leading a meeting, working on an important project, etc.).

2. Enter the situation in the second column.

3. In the last column, list as many specific actions you will take to deploy your chosen strategy. Personalize the strategy to increase your chances of successfully deploying the strategy.

4. After completing the table, answer the Discovery Questions.

Move Strategy	Situation	My Move Actions
EXAMPLE: Select or modify the situation when people can be emotionally and mentally present (consider day, time, and place)	Every Monday morning, I lead a team meeting, and everyone is already stressed thinking of the week ahead and not engaged	Instead of having the meeting Monday morning, I will move it to Tuesday morning, a less hectic time for all of us.
Select or modify the situation when people can be emotionally and mentally present (consider day, time, and place)		
Change the situation in the moment by moving meeting location, standing up, taking a break		
Match and Validate by recognizing how others feel		
Demonstrate an **Emotional Connection** by showing compassion and empathy		
Modulate tone of voice and pace of speech to get attention and shift the mood		
Provide a **distraction** away from the topic to a more neutral one (use rarely)		

Discovery Questions:

> WHAT MOVE STRATEGIES DID YOU TRY AND HOW EFFECTIVE WERE THEY?

> WHAT WAS CHALLENGING AND HOW CAN YOU MODIFY YOUR MOVE ACTIONS TO BE MORE EFFECTIVE?

> WHAT STRATEGIES WERE THE MOST DIFFICULT TO DEPLOY? WHY?

WHAT STRATEGIES ARE THE EASIEST FOR YOU? WHY?

WHAT OTHER ACTIONS CAN YOU TAKE TO MOVE OTHERS' EMOTIONS GOING FORWARD?

EMOTIONAL INTELLIGENCE BLUEPRINT

The four abilities of Emotional Intelligence (**Map, Match, Meaning, Move**), when considered together, form what we call the "Emotional Intelligence Blueprint". All four abilities are important to understand and practice individually, but the power of emotions is unleashed when you use them together. With practice, you will be able to look at challenges and be able to successfully resolve issues using the Blueprint. The following EI Blueprint exercises will help you view challenges as opportunities and strengthen your ability to solve challenges using the EI Blueprint. To build mastery, the exercises begin with an open-ended questions approach, followed by a more structured checklist approach and finally, ends with a 4-question format that we use in the Blueprint section of our books. Each person has their own method of creating an EI Blueprint, and we encourage you to use the one best suited for you.

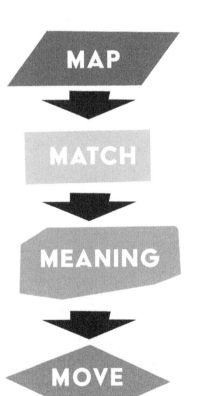

MAP — MAP YOUR FEELINGS AND OTHERS' FEELINGS

MATCH — MATCH FEELINGS TO CONNECT AND MATCH FEELINGS TO TASK

MEANING — UNDERSTAND THE MEANING OF THE FEELING(S) AND HOW THEY MAY CHANGE

MOVE — MOVE FEELINGS TO ACHIEVE IDEAL OUTCOMES

EI BLUEPRINT EXERCISE 1:
OPEN-ENDED QUESTIONS METHOD

Learning Objective: Emotions can arise for many reasons, at any moment, changing the dynamic of a conversation. At times, we may become overwhelmed by them, shut down or react ineffectively. This exercise helps you objectively witness emotions, deconstruct the events, and offer alternative solutions or resolving the issue using open-ended questions.

Instructions:

1. Watch the first three minutes of a scene from the movie Meet the Parents available on You Tube at: https://www.youtube.com/watch?v=6IOE4pN8Zro

2. Begin the Blueprint process with the desired outcome and goal for each person in the video (Step 1).

3. Map the emotions of the key people involved (Step 2).

4. Match the emotions to the task or goal (Step 3).

5. Determine Meaning of emotions for all parties and conduct what-if analyses (Step 4).

6. Consider move emotion strategies for all people involved (Step 5).

Step 1: The Desired Goal or Outcome

Desired Outcome/ Goal Question	Responses
What does each person want out of this situation?	
When this situation is resolved, what changes do they want to see in behaviors and thinking?	
What outcomes will they see when these changes happen?	
What goals will they achieve?	
What are the obstacles to achieving this outcome?	
How important is it to address this situation or to resolve the issue for each person?	
What does each person worry might happen?	
If they take action, what will they do if it doesn't work?	
If they do nothing, what will happen?	
How can any negative outcomes be prevented, or their effects reduced?	
What role can someone else play in achieving the best possible outcome?	
Who can assist them with this desired outcome?	

Step 2: Map Emotions

Usually when we complete a Blueprint it is because we are experiencing unpleasant emotions such as sadness, anger, boredom, frustration, loathing, etc., and we want to resolve the issue as soon as possible. As you watched the video, notice what is happening in their body and imagine their thoughts. Write down every emotion they are feeling regarding the situation—and feel free to note where you think they are feeling them in their body. It is possible you could be wrong in identifying other people's emotions because they are hiding their true feelings, or you may not be strong in this area of emotional intelligence. Regardless, write down what you believe the people are feeling about this situation.

Desired Outcome/ Goal Question	Responses
How is each person feeling about the situation now?	
How are they expressing their emotions related to this situation?	
How are others feeling about this situation?	
How are others expressing their emotions related to this situation?	
How certain are you that you accurately mapped their emotions?	
How might you be able to confirm your accuracy?	

Step 3: Match Emotions

Next, we move on to the second ability of emotional intelligence— the ability to Match the emotion to the goal or task at hand. As we noted earlier, research suggests certain emotions can facilitate certain tasks and problem solving. For example, if you want to have an end of year celebration, the emotions of joy, happiness and contentment are perfect for this occasion. And, if you have a looming deadline for an important project, perhaps the best emotions to achieve this task is anxiety, worry or sadness. When assessing this situation, determine which emotions would be best suited to accomplishing their goal or the task at hand. This is not how they feel about the task— the question is, which emotion(s) can help with the task?

Match Questions	Responses
Does it help them to feel this way? Why or why not?	
Which emotions are most helpful to address this issue?	
How much attention should they direct to the problem?	
Are their feelings guiding them in the right direction? Are they ignoring them or paying attention to their gut feel?	
Are they able to feel what the other person is feeling? Are they connecting with each other? To what degree? How do you know?	
How does the other person feel and think? How do they know?	
What is your guess as to the extent of their connection to each other?	

Step 4: Meaning of Emotions

Before taking action to Move your emotion to a more helpful one, it is important to get to the root cause of why people are feeling these emotions. If you skip this part of the Blueprint, you can go into problem solving mode without first addressing the underlying cause. Ask yourself, "Why do we feel the way we do? What happened to make people feel the way they do?" When we do this reflective work, it allows us to understand the real meaning of emotions. And it allows you to better understand the other person and see things from their perspective—or not! Finding the cause of emotions often leads to a better understanding of yourself and others. Determining the possible trajectory of the emotions you and others may experience is also critical as this allows you to predict how things could go wrong in unpleasantly charged situations.

Meaning Questions	Responses
Why does each person feel the way they do?	
What are the underlying causes for what they feel?	
Why do others feel the way they feel?	
What are the causes for others' emotions?	
How were they feeling before this situation happened?	
How did their feelings change, and why?	
List specific emotions they are feeling (list specific words.)	

Step 5: Move Emotions

Once you have acquired good emotional data by applying the first three abilities of emotional intelligence, you can now decide how to Move the emotions, the fourth emotional intelligence ability, to effectively achieve outcomes. Up until now you have been thinking of the challenge, the emotions others are experiencing, whether these emotions are helpful and what caused these emotions to arise. And while all these steps are important, it requires action to move emotions to a place best suited to resolve the issue at hand. Once you know what emotions are more helpful, and identify the root cause for the unpleasant emotions, what strategy will help others reach the optimal emotions to achieve the goals and outcomes they desire?

Review the Move strategies as outlined in MOVE EMOTION EXERCISE 3 of this workbook. After reviewing all the strategies, select the strategies you feel will work best for this situation and answer the following questions.

Move Questions	Responses
What are their feelings telling them about this situation?	
What strategies should they use to Move their emotions?	
How effective do you think the strategies you selected for each person would have been? What other strategies could be used?	

EI BLUEPRINT EXERCISE 2: CHECK LIST METHOD

Learning Objective: One way to resolve challenges is by answering emotionally intelligent questions as outlined in the previous exercise. This exercise is similar to Exercise 1 but instead of using open ended questions, it uses a check list approach to solving challenges. You may find this exercise easier, or more difficult, depending on your preference, but both methods are beneficial.

Instructions:

1. Watch the first three minutes of a scene from the movie Meet the Parents available on You Tube at: https://www.youtube.com/watch?v=6IOE4pN8Zro

2. After watching the video, analyze the passenger or the gate agent's behavior using the below steps. Place a "P" to indicate answers for the passenger and "G" for the gate agent next to the level of emotion demonstrated by each.

Step 1: Indicate the emotions experienced by each person. Annotate with an "A" for Agent and "P" for Passenger for each emotion you noticed during the encounter.

EMOTION	DO NOT FEEL <- -> STRONGLY FEEL			
ANGER	NONE	IRRITATED	FRUSTRATED	ANGRY
SADNESS	NONE	DOWN	SAD	DEPRESSED
SURPRISE	NONE	CURIOUS	SURPRISED	SHOCKED
SHAME	NONE	UNCOMFORTABLE	EMBARRASSED	ASHAMED
FEAR	NONE	CONCERN	WORRIED	AFRAID
PRIDE	NONE	CONFIDENT	ASSURED	PROUD
HAPPINESS	NONE	CONTENT	HAPPY	JOYOUS
EXCITEMENT	NONE	INTERESTED	EXCITED	ENTHUSIASTIC

How sure are you about the emotions you identified? How were these emotions expressed?

Step 2: Indicate the level of influence these emotions had on each person's thinking. Again, mark "A" for Agent and "P" for Passenger on each line.

<< Influence on Thinking >>										
Focused on details										Big picture
Accepting										Looking for a fight
Closed to ideas										Open to new ideas
Sees negatives										Sees positives
Fixed opinion										Easily persuaded
Slow, thoughtful										Quick to decide
Closed to bad news										Open to bad news

Step 3: Indicate the underlying causes of these emotions for the Agent and Passenger.

Causes of Emotions -- Agent		
ANGER	Obstacle or injustice	
SURPRISE	Unexpected event	
SADNESS	A loss	
FEAR	Impending threat	
DISGUST	Norms violated	
HAPPINESS	Gain something of value	

Causes of Emotions -- Passenger		
Anger	Obstacle or injustice	
Surprise	Unexpected event	
Sadness	A loss	
Fear	Impending threat	
Disgust	Norms violated	
Happiness	Gain something of value	

Step 4: How did each person sustain or move these emotions, and what would have been a better strategy? Refer to MOVE EXERCISE 3 to review examples of each emotional management strategy.

Managing the Situation	
How well did each person manage the situation?	
What strategies would be more effective?	

EI BLUEPRINT EXERCISE 3: BUILD YOUR OWN EI BLUEPRINT

Learning Objective: The Blueprint is a simple tool in principle, but like most simple ideas, it is difficult to apply well and consistently. To help you improve your leadership practices, this exercise will walk you through the process for creating your own Emotional Intelligence Blueprint using the open-ended questions approach. By using this approach, you can see challenges from different angles by taking different perspectives and being reflective about how the parties in the situation felt and how these feelings influenced their thinking and behaviors.

Instructions (each number aligns with the corresponding step):

1. Begin the Blueprint process with your desired outcome and goal.

2. Map the emotions of the key people involved.

3. Match the emotions to the task or goal.

4. Determine Meaning of emotions for all parties and conduct what-if analyses.

5. Consider move emotion strategies for all people involved.

6. Conduct an after-action review to get feedback and enhance EI skills.

Step 1: The Desired Goal or Outcome

Desired Outcome / Goal Question	Responses
What do I want out of this situation?	
When this situation is resolved, what changes do I want to see in behaviors and thinking?	
What outcomes will I see when these changes happen?	
What goals will we achieve?	
What are the obstacles to achieving this outcome?	
How important is it to address this situation or to resolve the issue for me?	
How important is it to address this situation or to resolve the issue for others?	
What do you worry might happen?	
If I take action, what will I do if it doesn't work?	
If I do nothing, what will happen?	
How can any negative outcomes be prevented, or their effects reduced?	
What role can I play in achieving the best possible outcome?	
Who can assist me with this desired outcome?	

Step 2: Map Emotions

Usually when we complete a Blueprint it is because we are experiencing unpleasant emotions such as sadness, anger, boredom, frustration, loathing, etc., and we want to resolve the issue as soon as possible. As you think of the challenge, do a body scan and notice what is happening in your body and in your thoughts. Write down every emotion you are feeling regarding the situation—and feel free to note where in your body you are feeling them.

Now we move on to how others are feeling. Your situation may involve one person, several people or a whole group of people. Take a moment to identify all the emotions you've noticed in others. It is possible you could be wrong in identifying the other person's emotions because they are hiding their true feelings, or you may not be strong in this area of emotional intelligence. Regardless, write down what you believe the other person is feeling about this situation

Map Questions	Responses
How do you feel about your challenge now?	
How are you expressing your emotions related to this situation?	
How are others feeling about this challenge?	
How are others expressing their emotions related to this situation?	
How certain are you that you accurately mapped the other person's emotions?	
How might you be able to confirm your accuracy?	
How did you feel during this interaction? (Answer this question if you are doing a post conversation analysis.)	

Step 3: Match Emotions

Next, we move on to the second ability of emotional intelligence— the ability to Match the emotion to the goal or task at hand. As we noted earlier, research suggests certain emotions can facilitate certain tasks and problem solving. For example, if you want to have an end of year celebration, the emotions of joy, happiness and contentment are perfect for this occasion. And, if you have a looming deadline for an important project, perhaps the best emotions to achieve this task is anxiety, worry or sadness. When assessing your challenge, determine which emotions would be best suited to accomplishing your goal or the task at hand. This is not how you and others feel about the task— the question is, which emotion(s) can help with the task?

Match Questions	Responses
Does it help you to feel this way? Why or why not?	
Which emotions are most helpful to address this issue?	
How much attention will you direct to the problem?	
Are your feelings guiding you in the right direction? Are you ignoring them or paying attention to your gut feel?	
Are you able to feel what the other person is feeling? Are you connecting with them? To what degree? How do you know?	
How does the other person feel and think? How do you know?	
What is your guess as to the extent of the other person's connection with you?	

Step 4: Meaning of Emotions

Before taking action to Move your emotion to a more helpful one, it's important to get to the root cause of why you and others are feeling these emotions. If you skip this part of the Blueprint, you can go into problem solving mode without first addressing the underlying cause. Ask yourself, "Why do I and others feel the way we do? What happened to make me, and others feel the way we do?" When we do this reflective work, it allows us to understand the real meaning of emotions. And it allows you to better understand the other person and see things from their perspective—or not! Finding the cause of emotions often leads to a better understanding of yourself and others. Determining the possible trajectory of the emotions you and others may experience is also critical as this allows you to predict how things could go wrong in unpleasantly charged situations.

Meaning Questions	Responses
Why do I feel this way?	
What are the underlying causes for what I feel?	
Why do others feel the way they feel?	
What are the causes for their emotions?	
How were you feeling before this situation happened?	
How did your feelings change, and why?	
How did the other person's feelings change and why?	
List specific emotions you and the others are feeling? (List specific words.)	

Step 5: Move Emotions

Once you have acquired good emotional data by applying the first three abilities of emotional intelligence, you can now decide how to Move the emotions, the fourth emotional intelligence ability, to effectively achieve your outcome. Up until now you have been thinking of your challenge, the emotions you and others are experiencing, whether these emotions are helpful and what caused these emotions to arise. And while all these steps are important, it now requires you to take action to move your emotions to a place best suited to resolve the issue at hand. Once you know what emotions are more helpful, and identify the root cause, what strategy will help you and others reach the optimal emotions to achieve the goals and outcomes you desire?

Review the Move strategies as outlined in MOVE EMOTION EXERCISE 3 of this workbook. After reviewing all the strategies for you and others, select the strategies you feel will work best for your situation and answer the following questions.

Move Questions	Responses
What are your feelings telling you about this situation?	
What strategies will you use to Move your emotions?	
What strategies will you use to Move others' emotions?	
How effective do you think the strategies you selected for yourself will be? What other strategies could be used?	
How effective do you think the strategies you selected for others will be? What other strategies could be used?	

Step 6: How did it go? Did you achieve your outcome or goal?

Things do not always work out how we planned. It is possible you achieved your desired outcome using these steps. Or, you could have achieved your desired outcome by changing the plan in real time. It is also possible something could have happened that prevented you from achieving your goal. Regardless of the outcome, it helps to refine your skills by getting feedback on how the goal was achieved and how people are feeling. If people are not feeling positive about the outcome, chances are the issue will resurface. Take some time for a Blueprint after-action review. These questions are for you, but ideally you will ask a trusted colleague these questions and listen to the answers.

Outcome & Analysis Questions	Responses
What happened as a result of the interaction?	
What did you want to happen?	
What worked well?	
What could you have done differently?	
Was there a better way to have handled it?	

Step 6: How did it go? Did you achieve your outcome or goal? (Continued)

Outcome & Analysis Questions	Responses
How satisfied were you with the outcome?	
How satisfied do you think the other person was with the outcome? How do you know?	
Are there any actions you could take now to result in a more productive outcome?	
What did you do that you would do again in a similar situation?	
How are you feeling now about the situation? Others?	
Do the emotions you or others are feeling set you up to continue positive working relationships?	

EI BLUEPRINT EXERCISE 4:
A STRUCTURED APPROACH TO BUILDING AN EI BLUEPRINT

Learning Objective: Some of us struggle with such broad, open-ended questions, especially as we develop the vocabulary of emotional intelligence and hone our skills. Oftentimes it is easier to use a more structured approach to creating Blueprints. This exercise provides steps to help guide you through the process.

Instructions:

Step 1: Identify Desired Goal:

First, consider your goal or objective and record it. Next, check the box which most closely matches your goal. Then, indicate what the other person's objective is and how you arrived at this conclusion.

	Desired Outcome or Goal
What is your goal or objective?	Your goal:
Which of these best matches your objective or goal?	A: Get other party to alter their position through assertion, criticism, and/or coercion B: Do not dwell on the issue, move past the issue and forget it C: Negotiate, understand, and persuade
What is the other person's goal or objective? How do you know?	Other person's goal and how I know:

Note that the strategies in the second column are oftentimes labeled confrontation (A), avoidance (B) and collaboration (C), respectively. In general, the EI Blueprint is based on collaborative strategies (C).

133

Step 2: Map Emotions

Next, indicate the emotions experienced by the person or people involved, including you (use initials for each person).

EMOTION	DO NOT FEEL <-		-> STRONGLY FEEL
ANGER	No	Irritated	Frustrated	Angry
SADNESS	No	Down	Sad	Depressed
SURPRISE	No	Curious	Surprised	Shocked
SHAME	No	Uncomfortable	Embarrassed	Ashamed
FEAR	No	Concern	Worried	Afraid
PRIDE	No	Confident	Assured	Proud
HAPPINESS	No	Content	Happy	Joyous
EXCITEMENT	No	Interested	Excited	Enthusiastic

How sure are you about the emotions you identified? How were these emotions expressed?

Step 3: Match Emotions

Next, indicate the influence these emotions had on each person. Place their initials in the appropriate block.

	<- Influence on Thinking ->							
Focused on details								Big picture
Accepting								Looking for a fight
Closed to ideas								Open to new ideas
Sees negatives								Sees positives
Fixed opinion								Easily persuaded
Slow, thoughtful								Quick to decide
Closed to bad news								Open to bad news

Now, indicate the extent of the felt connection between the people involved in this situation and what the feelings were like; that is, indicate the physical sensation each person experienced. Begin with the intensity of the emotional connection and then the overall feeling of the relationship. If there are more than two people involved, you can add them (feel free to include people's real names).

Relationship	Emotional Connection	Overall Feeling	
Person 1's emotional connection with Person 2	O Weak O Moderate O Strong	Warm Relaxed Sweet	Cold Tense Bitter
Person 2's emotional connection with Person 1	O Weak O Moderate O Strong	Warm Relaxed Sweet	Cold Tense Bitter

Step 4: Meaning of Emotions

Next, indicate the underlying causes of these emotions.

Meaning of Emotions			
To what extent are your feelings (Map) due to a mood (no major underlying event or cause) or to your current situation (Match)?	Mostly Mood	Both	Mostly Situation
To what extent are the feelings of the other person due to a mood or to the current situation?	Mostly Mood	Both	Mostly Situation
How did/will your emotions or feelings change if the situation continues?	Decrease	Same	Increase
How did/will the other person's emo- tions or feelings change if the situation continues?	Decrease	Same	Increase
What else do you think is the underlying cause of these emotions?			

Emotions have an identifiable cause and being clear about the underlying cause—a double check of sorts, can help you better address the situation. Next, we consider the underlying theme for basic emotions.

Causes of Emotions—You

Now consider the underlying theme or cause of the main emotions present in this situation for you. Indicate the exact event or cause for the emotion(s) experienced in this situation:

Emotion	Definition	Event
Anger	Obstacle or injustice	
Surprise	Unexpected event	
Sadness	A loss	
Fear	Impending threat	
Disgust	Norms violated	
Happiness	Gain something of value	

Causes of Emotions—Other Person

Now consider the underlying theme or cause of the main emotions present in this situation for the other person. Indicate the exact event or cause for the emotion(s) experienced in this situation:

Emotion	Definition	Event
Anger	Obstacle or injustice	
Surprise	Unexpected event	
Sadness	A loss	
Fear	Impending threat	
Disgust	Norms violated	
Happiness	Gain something of value	

Step 5: Move Emotions

This the last step in the emotional intelligence Blueprint. Determine which Move strategies would be most effective, and how you would implement them to reach a successful outcome. Be as specific as possible—this will increase the likelihood you will utilize these strategies and do so successfully. Refer to previous exercises for examples of each strategy.

Move Strategy - You	Implementation Notes: be specific about how you will implement
Prepare	
Modify Mood	
Reappraise	
Self-Talk	
Physiological	
Intervening Moment	
Express a Different Emotion	
Long Term	
Relationships	
Other	

Next, indicate which Move strategies for the other person would be most effective and how you would implement them. Be as specific as possible as this will increase the likelihood you will utilize these strategies successfully.

Strategy - Others	Implementation Notes: be specific about how you will implement
Distraction	
Select or Modify Situation	
Change Situation	
Emotional Connection	
Match and Validate	
Modulate Tone	
Physiological	
Express Concern	
Intervening Moment	
Other	

Remember, you do not have to select multiple Move strategies! Find the one you can implement and feel will be most effective in the situation.

Step 6: How Did It Go?

It is difficult to objectively evaluate our own skills and outcome. Ideally you would work with a mentor, coach, or colleague to debrief on how well it went. If you are unable to do this, then try to answer the "how did it go" question from your perspective, but also from the perspective of others involved and how they viewed the outcome.

How satisfied were you with the outcome?	O Not at all O Somewhat O Very O Extremely
How satisfied was the other person with the outcome?	O Not at all O Somewhat O Very O Extremely
Why were all parties extremely satisfied with the outcome?	
If all parties were not extremely satisfied, what would you do differently?	

EI BLUEPRINT EXERCISE 5:
BLUEPRINT DIFFICULT CONVERSATIONS

Learning Objective: Leaders need to set the example for others to follow and, therefore, it is important to prepare for difficult conversations. Emotions can often derail goals if they aren't helpful to the situation. This exercise helps prepare for difficult conversations so when the time arrives, you can handle the situation with emotional intelligence.

Instructions:

1. Think of a challenge you are currently facing and a difficult conversation you will need to have with another person, or multiple people.

2. Complete the blueprint before having the conversation.

3. After the conversation, describe the outcome and answer the Discovery Questions.

WHAT IS YOUR CURRENT CHALLENGE?

WHAT IS THE GOAL OF THE CONVERSATION?

EMOTIONAL INTELLIGENCE BLUEPRINT

MAP	**What are the emotions you and other are feeling?**
MATCH	**What emotions are the most helpful in the situation?**
MEANING	**What is the cause of the emotions (for you and the other person)?**
MOVE	**How will you sustain or move these emotions to have a better outcome?**

Discovery Questions:

WHAT WAS THE OUTCOME OF THE CONVERSATION?

WHAT EMOTIONS CAME UP DURING THE CONVERSATION FOR YOU AND THE OTHER PERSON?

WERE THESE EMOTIONS HELPFUL TO THE CONVERSATION? IF THEY WERE NOT, WHAT DID YOU DO TO MOVE THE EMOTION TO A MORE HELPFUL STATE?

IF THE CONVERSATION REACHED YOUR INTENDED GOAL – CONGRATULATIONS! IF IT DID NOT, WHAT WOULD YOU HAVE DONE DIFFERENTLY TO HAVE A BETTER OUTCOME?

WHAT DID YOU LEARN FROM COMPLETING THE BLUEPRINT ABOUT YOURSELF, THE OTHER PERSON, OR THE SITUATION?

EI BLUEPRINT EXERCISE 6:
DECONSTRUCTING EMOTIONAL SITUATIONS

Learning Objective: Unfortunately, there are times when you will not act in a highly emotionally intelligent manner. You acted in a way or said something that, when looking back, you regret. This exercise allows you to see different perspectives and strategies so that next time, you might have a better outcome.

Instructions:

1. Think of a difficult situation you encountered recently that was not handled well.

2. Use the EI Blueprint and answer each question to map out the difficult situation and possible Move strategies to reach your goal.

BREIFLY, DESCRIBE THE SITUATION

EMOTIONAL INTELLIGENCE BLUEPRINT

MAP	**What are the emotions you and other are feeling?**
MATCH	**What emotions are the most helpful in the situation?**
MEANING	**What is the cause of the emotions (for you and the other person)?**
MOVE	**How will you sustain or move these emotions to have a better outcome?**

WHAT WAS THE OUTCOME OF YOUR MEETING? WHAT WOULD YOU DO DIFFERENTLY NEXT TIME?

COMMITMENTS AND CONCLUSIONS

Congratulations on finishing the workbook, but you are not done with your work yet! To solidify your learning, it is important to commit to action and continue practicing and embedding emotional intelligence into your daily life. Practicing EI is challenging under the best circumstances and to do so effectively requires purpose, intention, and practice – lots of it. Take a moment to make a commitment to your continued growth by completing the remaining exercise.

MY COMMITMENTS TO ACTION

Consider the four emotional intelligence abilities from the previous exercises. What is one action, in each ability, you will commit to within the next thirty days to strengthen your relationships or enhance the effectiveness of your leadership? Sign and date this page and after 30 days, compare your actions to your commitments. If they matched, what was the outcome from your actions? If they did not, do not be discouraged and recommit to taking action. With intentional practice you will become an emotionally intelligent leader!

EI Ability	One Action I Will Take	Other People to Involve
Map to accurately identify emotions in myself and others		
Match emotions to the task at hand and practice emotional empathy		
Understand Meaning of emotion to identify root causes and improve relationships		
Move emotions in myself and others to build trust and reach goals		

AN EMOTIONALLY INTELLIGENT CONCLUSION

You picked up this workbook because you are in a class on EI, are being coached on EI or are curious about EI. We wrote this workbook for a broad audience and our guess is you found some of the exercises more or less difficult and more or less relevant to you. You probably skipped several exercises. Go back at some point to finish those exercises – especially the ones that seemed too difficult to complete at the time. There is a chance these developmental exercises could be of value to you.

We know all emotions matter and all emotions can be smart and helpful. The role of a highly emotionally intelligent leader is to access all emotions and match them to the task. However, you want to create a culture which generates a certain set of emotions to achieve organizational or personal goals. Do not forget this critical point!

Take a moment and indicate how you will generate the emotions listed in the table that will enable you and your organization to accomplish great things.

Emotion	My Actions
Engagement	
Respect	
Happiness	
Pride	
Appreciation	
Gratitude	
Inspiration	

APPENDICES

APPENDIX ONE - MOOD MAP

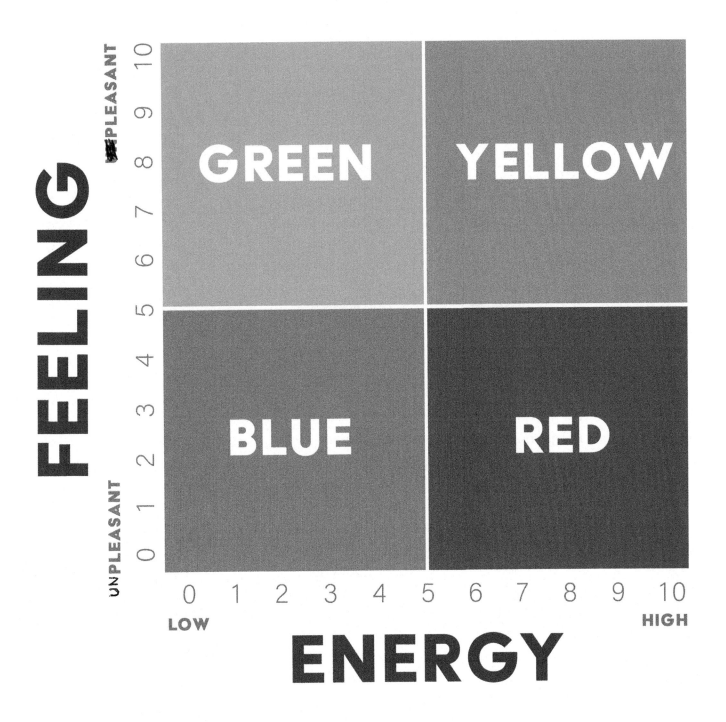

APPENDIX TWO - EMOTION WORDS

One of the goals of EI development is to expand our emotional vocabulary and to use the most precise and accurate word to describe feelings and emotions. This chart lists emotion and feeling words organized by Mood Map quadrant. Each word is given a Pleasantness (P) and Energy (E) rating from 1 to 10.

GREEN	P	E	BLUE	P	E	RED	P	E	YELLOW	P	E
acceptance	7	2	alienated	3	3	afraid	1	8	adoration	8	6
appreciative	7	4	apathy	2	3	aggravated	2	7	amazed	7	7
approval	7	4	bored	2	3	angry	2	8	anticipation	6	5
calm	7	1	confused	2	5	anguish	2	7	astonished	6	7
carefree	6	2	dejected	1	5	animosity	3	7	awe	6	7
comfortable	9	2	depressed	1	3	annoyed	3	7	blissful	8	6
committed	6	5	despondent	1	3	appalled	3	7	courageous	8	6
complacent	6	4	disappointed	1	3	apprehension	4	7	curious	6	6
composed	6	4	disapproval	1	4	contempt	2	6	delight	9	7
fond	8	5	distrust	1	5	embarrassed	3	6	enthusiastic	8	8
forgiveness	6	4	drowsy	3	3	envious	3	7	euphoric	7	9
fulfilled	8	4	ennui	3	3	exasperated	3	7	excited	8	9
grateful	9	3	fatigued	2	3	fear	1	8	exhilarated	8	9
gratitude	8	4	forlorn	3	4	frightened	3	8	exuberance	7	8
harmonious	9	4	gloomy	2	3	frustrated	2	6	glad	8	7
idyllic	6	4	grief	1	5	hate	1	9	glee	6	6
interested	6	5	guilt	2	4	hostile	2	9	included	7	5
like	6	3	hopeless	1	1	humiliating	2	7	inspired	9	7
nostalgic	5	3	isolation	2	3	indignant	3	6	jovial	7	6
peaceful	7	1	lonesome	3	2	irritable	3	8	joyful	10	7
placid	6	3	melancholic	2	2	loathe	1	7	laughter	8	6
pleasant	9	3	miserable	1	3	nervous	3	7	lively	7	8
protected	7	3	morose	2	5	obnoxious	2	6	love	10	6
relaxed	7	2	mourning	2	4	outraged	2	7	merry	8	7
relieved	8	3	pessimistic	2	3	overwhelmed	3	7	mirth	8	6
respectful	8	4	regretful	2	4	panic	2	9	motivated	9	6
restful	7	1	regrettable	2	3	rage	1	9	optimistic	9	6
satisfaction	9	5	rejected	1	4	remorse	2	6	passion	8	8
satisfying	8	5	resentful	2	5	repulsive	2	7	pleased	9	5
secure	7	3	sad	2	3	restless	3	7	proud	8	7
serenity	8	1	shame	1	5	scared	3	7	rejoice	7	6
submissive	8	1	sorrow	1	1	shocked	2	8	sanguine	6	6
thankful	9	3	sullen	3	3	spiteful	1	7	surprise	7	8
thoughtful	6	2	tired	3	2	terrified	1	9	thrilled	8	8
tranquil	8	1	unhappy	1	4	vigilance	4	6	valued	8	6
trust	8	5	worthless	1	3	worried	2	8	vibrant	7	8

APPENDIX THREE - EMOTION FAMILIES

Words from Appendix Two, as well as additional words, are listed below grouped by six, basic emotion families in order of intensity (energy).

ANGER	DISGUST	FEAR	HAPPY	SAD	SURPRISE
skepticism	disapproval	concern	contentment	thoughtfulness	anticipation
irritation	distaste	worry	peace	pensiveness	curiosity
annoyance	aversion	anxiety	confidence	disappointment	surprise
frustration	objection	agitated	pleasure	boredom	wonderful
criticism	hesitancy	alarmed	optimism	loneliness	astonished
insecurity	avoidance	afraid	power	abandonment	stunned
indignation	disgust	overwhelm	pride	desperation	amazed
jealousy	repulsion	panic	happiness	apathy	shocked
hurt	loathing	terror	playfulness	emptiness	
resentment			delight	guilt	
threat			elation	distress	
violation				shame	
fury				grief	
rage				misery	

ABOUT THE AUTHORS

DAVID R. CARUSO, PhD

David is the co-founder of Emotional Intelligence (EI) Skills Group. In addition, he is a research affiliate at the Yale Center for Emotional Intelligence and Senior Advisor in the Yale College Dean's Office. David is the co-author of the Mayer, Salovey, Caruso Emotional Intelligence Test (MSCEIT). He and colleague Peter Salovey wrote The Emotionally Intelligent Manager, and he is a co-author of The Anchors of Emotional Intelligence school program (Brackett, Caruso & Stern). David has published numerous articles – peer reviewed journal articles, reviews and chapters - on the topics of emotional intelligence and leadership. He has trained thousands of professionals around the world, from Japan to Brazil.

David received his PhD in psychology from Case Western Reserve University and was awarded a two-year postdoctoral fellowship in psychology at Yale University.

David has also held positions in market research, strategic planning, and product management, led numerous product development teams, conducted sales training seminars, developed and implemented marketing plans and introduced new products in the United States and Europe.

Contact: david@eiskills.com

LISA T. REES, PCC, MPA

Lisa is an experienced leader, coach and instructor with the U.S. Citizenship and Immigration Services (USCIS). Having worked over three decades for USCIS (legacy Immigration and Naturalization Service), Lisa led teams in implementing financial systems and cost efficiencies throughout her agency before switching career fields to become a certified leadership coach in 2015.

Lisa has an A.S. in Accounting and a B.S. in Management from Champlain College and her Master in Public Administration from Norwich University. Lisa is certified in the MSCEIT as well as certified in Appreciative Inquiry (AI) and numerous leadership assessment tools Lisa is a strategic partner with the David L. Cooperrider Center of Appreciative Inquiry and teaches EI and AI at the Naval Postgraduate School.

In addition to working for USCIS, Lisa has her own leadership consulting and coaching practice, LTR Leadership, where she provides consulting, facilitates workshops and coaches executives and their teams using EI and AI as the foundation for her practice. This is Lisa's third book and she has written several journal articles on EI and AI.

Contact: lisa@ltrleadership.com.

ACKNOWLEDGEMENTS

We would like to acknowledge the seminal work of **John (Jack) Mayer** and **Peter Salovey**. Their theories and research are the inspiration for our workbook. They have not endorsed this content and all errors or misapplication of theory are the authors.

John Millburn was the first facilitator to field test the materials and his feedback was invaluable.

Rachel Norton and **Jeff Abeling** provided proofreading and editing assistance.

Caitlyn Kenney designed and produced the layout of the workbook.

Adam Robinson of *Good Book Developers* managed the book production process for us.

Without their assistance, and the support of our families, this workbook would not have been possible.